BITTEN BY THE DANCE BUG

A Parent's Guide to Recreational and Competitive Dance

First Edition:
Published by
Windmill Consulting LLC
P.O. Box 62519
Colorado Springs, CO 80962

Printed in the U.S.A.

bittenbythedancebug.com
info@bittenbythedancebug.com

Library of Congress Control Number: 2018901041
ISBN Number: 978-0-692-93964-2

Cover and Interior Design by Konstance Frey at SANDIA Advertising
Edited by Hailey Olson

Cover images also appear inside the book with credits.

To my husband Will, I couldn't have done this without you. And I wouldn't have wanted to.

To Jill, you are the daughter of my dreams, the one that made all my dreams come true.

To all the dance moms and dads who support their
children's pursuit of dance, I salute your commitment and sacrifice.

TABLE OF CONTENTS

"I keep on dancing—until there is only...the dance."

— MICHAEL JACKSON

© Can Stock Photo / refocusphoto

INTRODUCTION

Somewhere, somehow, the idea of enrolling your child in a dance lesson is born. Maybe you were a dancer in your youth; you've seen a neighbor or family member participate in recital; you want your child to try an enjoyable, extra-curricular activity; or your child approaches you, expressing an interest in taking up dance. Whatever the reason that got you to this point, you are now connected to the world of dance. And you don't mind. You know dance is a remarkable thing—one of the best things, in fact, that children could ever get themselves into.

Initially, no students of dance knows how far their feet and heart might take them. A child may be "bitten by the dance bug," and a general interest ultimately becomes a passion. That part-time recreational dancer who dabbles in dance as a hobby can evolve into a committed recreational or competitive dancer. This evolution requires knowledge, as well as physical, mental, financial, and emotional commitment that parents don't usually anticipate. A friend of mine recently said, "as our daughter became passionate about dance, we were flying blind."

I've been there. I'm a dance mom. My daughter, husband, and I have faced this adventure together for a decade, from our first steps into a dance studio to the spectacular, fierce world of competition. It's been a thrill of a ride (to say the least), with its highs, lows, and everything in between!

At the beginning of our dance journey, we didn't know many things—and worse, we hadn't a clue of how much we didn't know. We had no idea how many details, layers, and nuances exist within a child's dance world. The recipe for success wasn't tied together with a neat bow and presented to us. We often found ourselves wishing that we'd been more prepared before diving in head-first. Our learning curve involved both first-hand knowledge based on our experiences—including our fair share of lessons, trials, and errors—combined with information gleaned from studio staff, respective literature and online resources, fellow friends in the dance community, and the dancers themselves. After all this time, we continue to observe, learn, and evolve.

Once I felt that our family had a reasonable grasp on the subject matter, I reflected on our experience and wondered if there was something we could have done (or could have had) that might have eased the learning process. I realized that having a consolidated, thorough guide would have been extremely valuable when facing countless situations and decisions during the pursuit of our daughter's passion for dance.

But it's never too late—and hindsight, as they say, is 20/20. I'm therefore sharing the knowledge gathered from our experience in hopes that others may benefit from it as they travel their own dance journey.

Geared toward the dance-oriented development of children aged 2-18 gained at local dance studios, the information within this book is intended to help you prepare for and traverse the beautiful, complex world of dance. While my perspective is influenced by the experience of our daughter, most of the information herein can apply to male dancers, as well.

Photo Credit - JCM Photography

To relate to a wide range of prospective and current dancers, this guide is organized into two main sections:

RECREATIONAL DANCE
for the Younger Dancer and the Evolving Dancer

COMPETITIVE DANCE
for the Advanced Dancer

WITHIN THIS BOOK, YOU WILL LEARN

- Practical dance basics including dance genres, dress code, level progression, and the importance of technique.
- Factors to consider when choosing a dance studio regarding its recreational and competitive dance programs.
- All aspects of dance recitals.
- Insight into expenses—time, energy, and costs.
- The ins-and-outs of competitions and conventions.
- Ideas for managing relationships with studio staff and other parents and dancers.
- Tips to enhance the dance experience.

No matter what type of dance program interests your child, it's important to have timely and relevant information. Educating yourself as a dance parent is an excellent first step in removing uncertainty and places you in a stronger position to plan and deal with whatever comes your way.

Whatever their level of involvement and achievement with dance, children will learn positive lessons that apply to all aspects of life. Regardless of the type and length of a dancer's study, it always begins with a first step…

BENEFITS OF DANCE

Before diving into the details of a child's dance world, take a moment to note—and truly consider—dance's numerous potential benefits. Whether manifesting as a low-priority hobby or a time-consuming passion, participating in the dance scene rewards a child with a wealth of characteristics and attributes that will prove useful within and beyond both childhood and academia (e.g., extra-curricular activities, sports, and a multitude of career paths).

Dance participation, whether recreational or competitive within a company[1] structure, proves instrumental for

- Developing stamina, muscle tone, strength, and flexibility.
- Developing poise, coordination, and postural control.
- Developing musicality and an "ear" for music, beat, and rhythm.
- Improving memory and sequential ordering by learning combinations and choreography.
- Establishing a lifelong respect and appreciation for dance and the arts in general.
- Cultivating mental strength and discipline by developing performance skills, a knowledge of stage presence, time management skills, and self-discipline.
- Learning how to make a positive first impression, and how to handle competition or conflicting interests.
- Engaging in a discipline that is both individual and team-oriented.
- Learning how to work toward common goals as set by a competition team.
- Cultivating discipline, vision, and a strategic mindset in terms of setting and achieving goals through hard work, determination, and training.
- Learning to work with different types of personalities and forming bonds of friendship with peers.
- Developing leadership skills by becoming a role model for younger dancers, as well as by leading choreographies, assisting in teaching sessions, and helping nurture newcomers in the studio.
- Embracing the community and becoming part of a globally-acclaimed performance art that has no geographical boundaries and has the power to transcend languages and cultures.
- Cultivating a sense of purpose, pride, and belonging by becoming a part of something larger than oneself.

[1] For the purposes of this book, "company" herein will be used to imply a dance "company," "team," "line," or "troupe."

"Dance is the hidden language of the soul, of the body." — MARTHA GRAHAM

Photo Credit - Danielle Trina Photography

© Can Stock Photo / MilanMarkovic

SECTION 1: RECREATIONAL DANCE

RECREATIONAL DANCE provides basic developmental instruction that is focused on technique, strength, flexibility, and performance skills. Students will develop through proficiency levels based on their technical and physical aptitude, maturity, dedication, and mental preparedness. Some of the most common genres of recreational dance include classical ballet, tap, jazz, contemporary, lyrical, modern, musical theater, hip hop, acrobatics (nicknamed "acro"), and pointe.

In this section for the Recreational Dancer—for young dancers (2-5 years old) and evolving dancers (6+ years old) — we'll examine

- **General information** regarding dance studios.
- How to **select a dance studio.**
- Typical **dress code** or **uniform requirements**.
- How **dance recitals** are typically planned and carried out.
- The variety of **dance classes/genres.**
- What **dance technique** entails—and why it is the underpinning of ongoing success.
- **Level proficiency and progression**.
- **Injury prevention** and care.
- Estimated **annual costs.**

> *"Dance is the most fundamental of all art forms. If a thing moves, it lives. And we have dance all around us."*
>
> — TWYLA THARP

"Dance is music made visible."

— GEORGE BALANCHINE

GENERAL STUDIO INSIGHT

Like every business, **each studio** is geared toward a specific market and **will offer unique dance programs.** Below is a brief review of **general dance studio information** for the recreational (nicknamed "rec") dancer. An **in-person site visit** is, of course, the primary and best way to understand a studio's management structure, programmatic emphasis, facilities, and overall culture. Having educated yourself about key points of interest beforehand, you will arrive better prepared, knowing what questions to ask and what to look for.

STUDIO STAFF ROLES

Before signing up with a dance studio, it's helpful to understand the responsibilities of the staff and align your expectations accordingly. The dance instructor (also called "teacher") is the person with whom your child will interact most in the studio. The chemistry between teacher and student will greatly influence a child's overall class experience. There are others who will play significant roles in your child's recreational dance training, including the studio owner, office manager, and directors. All studio staff members become role models for the students whom they guide and teach.

Although not every studio will be structured the same, for explanatory purposes, the below diagram models **a common organization chart for medium to large-sized dance studios**, followed by common responsibilities associated with each staff role.

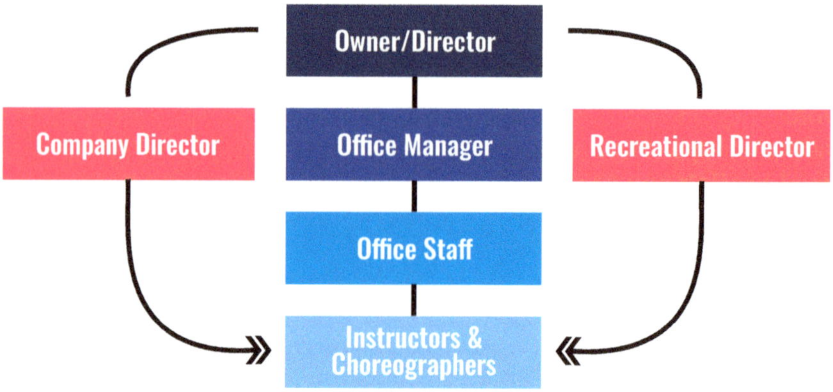

THE OWNER/DIRECTOR

- Manages the overall financial health of the business.
- Manages all legal obligations, accounts payable, and payroll.
- Manages student enrollment levels, customer satisfaction, and studio reputation in the community.
- Manages the studio facilities.
- Conceptualizes, plans, and implements the artistic vision and direction of the dance studio.
- Hires, manages, and nurtures the company director, recreational director, office manager, instructors, and choreographers.
- Produces annual performance events (e.g., recitals).
- Plans and implements marketing strategies.
- May fulfill the role of instructor and/or choreographer.
- May fulfill the role of recreational director and/or company director.

THE OFFICE MANAGER

- Is the face you see each day behind the desk in the lobby of the studio.
- Handles customer service, including answering phone calls and in-person questions.
- Is the go-to person for registration, scheduling, tuition and billing, and release forms.
- Informs families of calendar events, recital information, studio closure information, and other news by sending out newsletters and updating the company website and social media accounts.
- Troubleshoots issues that may arise and, as necessary, directs issues to the appropriate staff member.

THE RECREATIONAL DIRECTOR

- Oversees the recreational training program implementation.
- May fulfill the role of instructor and/or choreographer.

THE COMPANY DIRECTOR

- Plans and manages the company (competitive) program (e.g., auditions, competition and convention events, guest choreographers, company rehearsal schedules, etc.), oversees choreographers, company team members, and related activities.
- Ensures competition dances are entered in the appropriate categories (e.g., age, entry level, performance level), approves costume and song choices made by the choreographer.
- May fulfill the role of instructor and/or choreographer.

© Can Stock Photo / HighwayStarz

THE INSTRUCTOR

- Plans and leads dance training classes for individuals or groups of dancers in a particular style or technique such as ballet, tap, jazz, contemporary, lyrical, modern, musical theater, hip hop, acro, and pointe.
- Choreographs class recital routines.
- Is a role model for children.
- May fulfill the role of choreographer.

THE CHOREOGRAPHER

- Creates individual and group dance routines and performances; selects the genre, song, costumes, and props. These performances can include recital, showcase, and competition pieces.
- May fulfill the role of instructor.

© Can Stock Photo / HighwayStarz

THE DANCE YEAR: DAYS AND HOURS OF OPERATION

A dance year generally aligns with the academic school year, starting in August or September and ending in May or June of the following year.

COMMON RECREATIONAL DANCE YEAR

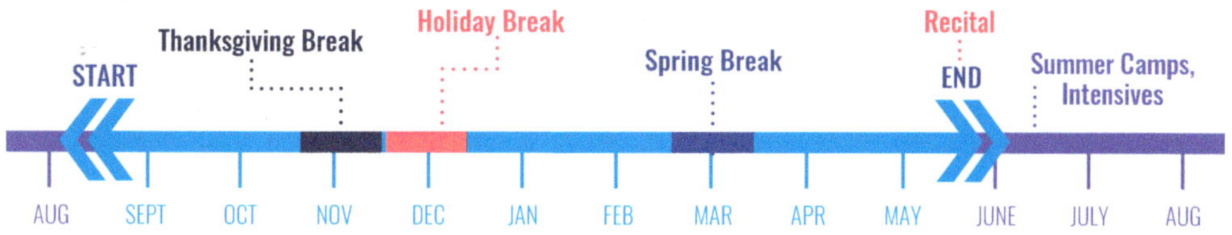

Although this is a common timeline, studios and regions will vary. In certain regions, for example, the recreational dance year runs eight months, starting in September and ending with recital in April.

DURING WINTER, SPRING, AND SUMMER BREAKS (aligned with academia), most studios are closed for normal business (i.e., recreational classes). During these periods, many studios will offer opportunities which supplement regular classes during the dance year. This can be an excellent time for

- Young dancers to participate in themed “camps” which introduce or celebrate the art of dance in a fun atmosphere.
- New students to try out classes before making a long-term commitment.
- Committed students to maintain their dance fitness by taking intensives and other supplementary training classes.

For **younger dancers (2-5 years old),** classes are generally offered in the morning and early afternoon hours, Monday through Saturday. For **older dancers (6+ years old)**, studio hours will typically start after the academic school day and run through the late evening, Monday through Friday. On Sundays, studios are usually closed for normal business.

	Monday	Tuesday	Wednesday	Thursday	Friday	Saturday	Sunday
Morning/Early Afternoon 9AM-3PM	Young Dancers (2-5 years old)					Young, Older Dancers	Typically closed, but may be open for individual lessons or rehearsals for competitive dancers.
Late Afternoon/ Early Evening 3:30-6:30PM	Young (2-5 years old) and Older Dancers (6+ years old)					Closed	
Late Evening 6:30-9:30PM	Older Dancers (6+ years old)				Closed	Closed	

Sample schedule for dance students

CLASS SIZE

The number of students in a dance class tends to directly influence the quality of instruction and quantity of time spent on each child. It’s common sense that a **smaller class size allows teachers to allocate time and energy more abundantly to each dancer,** dedicate more time and attention towards teaching proper technique, and ensure the wellness and safety of the children. A teacher can be much more personable and focused towards a class of 10 students as opposed to a class of 30.

An appropriate class size generally depends on the **age of the students, dance genre, instructor, and space availability (room size).** Although not all dance professionals a children would be 8-10 students; for grade-school students, who need less supervision and who have better individual focus, a class size of 12-15 students would be appropriate.

Good studios are careful with their student-teacher ratios to ensure that instructors aren't overwhelmed and students don't feel neglected. If class sizes are beyond what's recommended or effective, **an assistant may be asked to support the instructor, or the class will be split into two.** On the other hand, if too few students are enrolled in a class, the studio may decide to combine it with another class or cancel it altogether.

EXPENSES AND PAYMENTS

For planning purposes, it's helpful to be aware of the expenses related to recreational dance:

- **Annual registration fee** (payable to the dance studio when enrolling in classes and covers administrative costs)
- **Class tuition** (payable monthly to the dance studio)
- **Dance attire,** including clothes and footwear (purchased at the studio or through local and online retailers)
- **Recital** and **holiday performance** expenses, including fees that pay for facility rental, security, lighting, clean-up, costumes, and tickets for participating guests (all payable to the dance studio)

The more recreational classes your child takes, the higher the expenses—of tuition, dance attire, and recital—can be.

Dance studios may offer **discounts** (especially in terms of tuition) in the following scenarios:

- **Tiered pricing** for when a student enrolls in more than one class (i.e., multiple-class discounts, reducing the monthly tuition fee per class as the number of classes increases)
- When offering an **unlimited dancer package** (i.e., monthly tuition is capped for an unlimited number of classes/hours per dancer)
- When offering an **unlimited family package** (i.e., monthly tuition is capped for an unlimited number of classes/hours per family)
- When the **tuition for the entire year is paid upfront** (e.g., a 10% discount to the overall expense)
- For **early-bird registration** (e.g., a 15% discount for families who register before a certain date)
- When offering **free trial lessons**
- For **active military families or other special categories** (e.g., waiving the registration fee and/or offering tuition discounts)
- When rewarding **referrals** (i.e., offering credit or bonus points to the account of a current dance family for referring new students)

Example of Tiered Pricing

Hrs/Week	Monthly Tuition
1	$50.00
2	$97.00
3	$142.00
4	$185.00
5	$225.00
6	$262.00
Unlimited Dancer:	$275.00
Unlimited Family:	$350.00

ONLINE SYSTEMS

Although not applicable to all dance studios, many use **web-based business management software to manage customer accounts including registration, tuition, billing, class attendance, and appointments.** Such tools include automated payments, and text and email reminders—among other helpful functionality—and reduce the administrative burden of both studio staff and dance families. For parents, having an overview of scheduled, upcoming payments as well as historical transactions is extremely valuable.

COMMUNICATION AND AGREEMENT POLICIES

Studios tend to keep their students and respective families informed through monthly newsletters and updates—via email, a company website, or social media—with time-sensitive information regarding classes, events, schedules, recitals, costumes, studio closures, and more. **Customizable smartphone applications** are becoming more widely used by dance studios.

Studios may hold an **orientation meeting** at the beginning of the dance season to introduce parents and children to studio staff and provide an overview of events, policies, dress code requirements, communication methods, expectations, and volunteer opportunities. This forum would be a time for parents to ask questions and gather any information they need. It's intended to ensure a smooth transition into studio life.

A dance studio's **communication policy** can be very specific. Understanding and following the policy increases the likelihood of obtaining timely information and will contribute to a positive interaction with the staff. Instructors of younger dancers tend to make themselves more accessible to parents. However, a general rule of thumb is that—except for emergencies—**parents should not approach teachers during or between classes**; it's almost always discouraged and usually frowned upon. Some studios don't allow parents and students to phone teachers directly. Others ask that email (not phone calls or social media messages) be used to communicate with staff.

If you have general questions (e.g., class scheduling, tuition and billing, calendar events, and school closures), bring them first to the **Office Manager** at the front desk who should be able to provide you with answers and necessary information. If you have specific needs or desires that affect your child's dance lesson, follow the instructor's preferred method of communication as outlined in the studio's overall communication policy.

"I've been dancing since I was seven years old. It wasn't until eight years later that I learned I had a 75% hearing loss. During this time, I didn't realize why I wasn't able to hit the beat of the music or be in synch with the other dancers. One of teachers was tuned into my struggles and helped me. Instead of counting the beat, she would put certain steps to certain words in the song lyrics which would allow me to align the steps with the counts and have better timing. This time was so challenging for me that I almost considered quitting dance, which was a devastating thought because dance was my life. Once I realized I had a hearing issue, I was given hearing aids and heard simple sounds such as the wind and hearing a bird chirp for the first time. I was also able to dance to the beat of the music. Even though my disability challenged me, through my experience with dance, I now have the confidence to know that I can push through the struggles of life." - Gillie Tate, Dancer

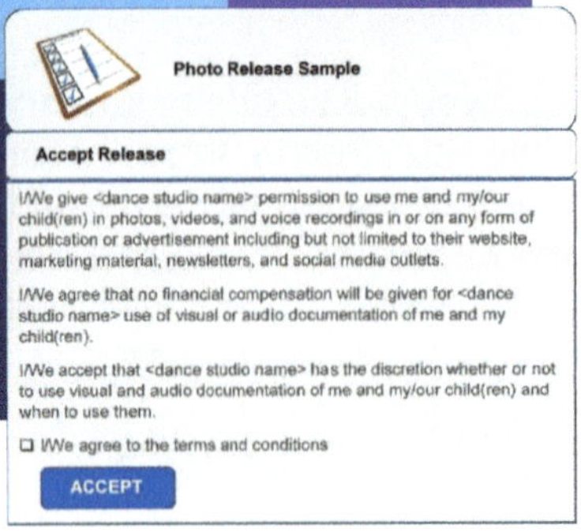
Photo Release Sample

Accept Release

I/We give <dance studio name> permission to use me and my/our child(ren) in photos, videos, and voice recordings in or on any form of publication or advertisement including but not limited to their website, marketing material, newsletters, and social media outlets.

I/We agree that no financial compensation will be given for <dance studio name> use of visual or audio documentation of me and my child(ren).

I/We accept that <dance studio name> has the discretion whether or not to use visual and audio documentation of me and my/our child(ren) and when to use them.

☐ I/We agree to the terms and conditions

ACCEPT

Dance studios typically require parents to sign a **general release form** which releases and discharges the studio from any liability or claims of physical injury during the child's time at the studio. You may also be asked to sign a **photo release** granting the studio permission to publish images of your child for marketing purposes. Although most people welcome the opportunity to see their child's face in a brochure or a website, the right of granting permission remains the parent's.

COMMUNITY SERVICE

As a hub of sociable activity, many **dance studios tend to participate in local community outreach activities** for a number of reasons. It's an excellent way to establish a presence and network in the region while also contributing—in whatever way and to whatever extent—to the betterment of society. Community outreach also positively impacts the dancers who are included in these events, since it exposes and encourages them to join in by servicing their community (even if that's just by putting a smile on people's faces and cheering them up!). Dancers can become more thoughtful, well-rounded, compassionate individuals who begin to realize the need and power of making a difference.

Such community outreach programs may include visits to local retirement homes or hosting events to raise money for charities and other important causes. They may host charity performances and "adopt" families in need, especially during the holiday season in December. This is **an opportunity for dancers to give back to the community,** instilling in them a sense of purpose and excitement.

As a parent, note that there may be **associated expenses** (e.g., costume costs for a holiday performance) for participation. Check with the studio to understand whether participation is **optional or required** and what the anticipated costs are. Weigh the costs while considering the aforementioned benefits.

Holiday performance at retirement home

Dancers supporting the National Down Syndrome Society's buddy walk

Photo Credit - Renee Garcia

Photo Credit - JCM Photography

STUDIO SELECTION STRATEGY FOR THE RECREATIONAL DANCER

If you're ready to enroll your child in a recreational dance program, one question will immediately come to mind: How do I find a good studio for my child? It's wise to be proactive and informed when choosing a place for your child to participate in his or her very first lesson. He or she might get "bitten by the dance bug" and you may find yourself in need of a dance "home" for the long run.

For the younger dancer (2-5 years old), local dance studios should offer classes that are age-appropriate—maybe a "Combo" (Ballet/Tap), a "Tap and Twist," a "Tippy Toes," or a "Mommy and Me" class. These classes are geared toward creating a positive, fun, and nurturing environment where children can develop gross motor skills, listening skills, and musicality while exploring their creativity. **For older dancers (6+ years old),** you will discover that most recreational dance classes are based on genre, skill level, and age. Typically, these classes will place emphasis on classical training, proper classroom etiquette, and choreography.

Every dance studio has its own personality and atmosphere. The first time you walk into one, you may experience the delightful, high energy whirling within the space—kids getting ready for class, parents chatting, students dancing to music inside enclosed rooms with glass windows for observation, and so on. You can get a sense of the overall environment by paying close attention to people's attitudes. Do the teachers seem experienced and friendly? Do the parents and students generally appear relaxed, comfortable, and happy within this environment? Do you have a sense that this studio combines characteristics of quality and compassion?

Even though your child may start out with a single class that doesn't yet seem relevant for a young dancer, keep in mind that **selecting the right dance studio is an important decision from both an educational dance perspective and a cultural perspective.** Ideally, the studio is an environment that you, and especially your child, will be exposed to on a recurring basis. Your child will learn lessons, forge friendships, and master habits in this space. **The setting matters.**

"When you wish upon a star, you just might become one."
— PAULA ABDUL

QUALITY TRAINING & STUDIO CULTURE

Quality training is extremely important—especially in the long run—and is an essential ingredient for your child to eventually attain his or her full potential. Bad habits are very difficult to undo. For that reason, some experts argue that it's better for a child to start training later in a more qualified environment than to form bad habits from early, subpar training. The studio **culture**—principles, values, and beliefs—becomes an important dynamic in a dancer's life and must not be underestimated on both an individual and collective level. Upon enrolling your child, you'll become part of a culture, one where staff, families, and dancers will continue to grow together, while sharing a history and a vision. Your relationship with them will develop over time. The initial class for your child may develop into a larger commitment where these relationships and the studio culture become cornerstones in your child's growth and development, as well as your family's overall experience.

TAKING STEPS TO ENROLL YOUR CHILD IN A STUDIO

1. DO YOUR RESEARCH

- Take the time to survey local studios in your area for comparison and assessment purposes.
- Gather references from family, friends, neighbors, or your child's school.
- Visit studio websites and social media to get a better sense of who they are and what's important to them.
- Read and evaluate online customer reviews.

2. TAKE A TRIP

- Visit each facility that interests you. Although dropping in is typically acceptable, it may not yield the results you desire since availability of studio staff may be limited or key personnel may be absent. **Making appointments will ensure that time is dedicated to you.**
- Consider the safety of the facility and location. Is the general area safe? Is there a qualified adult in the reception area? Are there security cameras?
- Seek professionalism in the studio staff.
- Seek cleanliness and overall organization in the facility.
- Discuss schedule, costs, and commitments including recital.
- Seek input from dance families already attending the studio.
- Learn about ways to observe your child during classes (e.g., via viewing windows or a CCTV system noted in more detail on page 14)—especially important for parents of young dancers.
- Don't be shy about asking questions (e.g., How long have you been in business? What is the experience of your instructors? Why should I choose your dance studio over another?)
- Ask about any discounts that may be available (e.g., for active military families).
- Ask about free trial classes, a free sample week, or an at-no-extra-charge "bring-a-friend" week to determine which classes might be right for your child.
- Learn about typical class sizes and student–teacher ratios.

- Learn how and when class level placements are determined—especially important for evolving dancers (6+ years old). (Refer to **Level Progression on** page 53 to learn more.)
- Inquire about the dance floors in the context of injury prevention. Are they "sprung" or "floating" to absorb the impact of a dancer's repetitive movements and long hours of dance? Is the surface of the floors made of vinyl composite or "Marley," which helps control a dancer's slipping?
- Ask if you can take home a copy of a recital DVD from the previous year.
- Assess the quality of training, background, and experience of instructors.
- Inquire whether the studio participates in any community outreach activities.

3. COMPARE AND DECIDE

- Compare location, costs, schedule, class size, training, and the studio's overall culture and environment.
- Select the studio that aligns with you and your child's interest (e.g., Ballet School vs. a dance studio with a variety of dance genres).
- **Pay attention to your gut feeling** when you visit a studio. A first impression counts much more than you might think. If a studio doesn't feel right for both you and your child, trust your instincts!
- While it might seem like a simple or insignificant decision now, take into account that a dance studio is an environment in which your child will grow, learn, play, achieve, and hopefully thrive—both as a dancer and as an individual. Remember, too, that proper training for serious dancers is extremely important in reaching their potential.

Since each studio has its own unique culture, staff, and offerings it's okay to try multiple studios (if you have that option in your area) before settling on one of them for the longer term. **Just because one studio isn't a good fit for your child doesn't mean you can't find another one that is.**

Photo Credit
King Shots, Inc.

Photo Credit - JCM Photography

"Kennedy has Down syndrome... that means, among other things, that she has to work harder to accomplish things than her typical peers. It's important that she has people who believe in her and push her to be the very best Kennedy she can be in every area of her life.

When she learned to walk, she ran. When she learned to run, she danced. When she learned to dance, she flew. Her wings were given to her by the dance teachers who believe in her." — **Renee Garcia, Kennedy's mom**

Photo Credit - JCM Photography

© iStock Photo / Steven Debenport

"My mother told me I was dancing before I was born. She could feel my toes tapping wildly inside her for months." – GINGER ROGERS

SPECIFIC TO THE YOUNGER DANCER (2-5 YEARS OLD)

Younger dancers (2-5 years old) —also known as **"minis," "newbies," or "petites"**—will generally take a single class per week on a month-to-month basis and many will participate in the annual recital event. While some of these children take classes and perform on stage full of enthusiasm, others will be shy and frightened—expect a variety of reactions to these new environments and people, including instructors, other dancers, and an audience. In any case, the innocence of these young dancers is something to marvel at.

Don't be discouraged if your dancer has a tough time during his or her first dance lesson. Some instructors even say it can take up to 3-6 lessons for a young dancer to get acclimated and comfortable within this new setting.

Some children at the upper range of this age category may already be "bitten by the dance bug" and have the interest and necessary skills to be on a competition team!

© Can Stock Photo Inc. / Vanell

© Can Stock Photo Inc. / parislatrell

SELECTING THE IDEAL DANCE STUDIO

Below are **overarching factors for parents of young dancers** when choosing a dance studio for their child:

LOCATION

Proximity of a dance studio to your home, school, office, or grandparents is typically the first consideration you will make when selecting a place for your child to take dance lessons. Along with convenience, the reigning characteristic should be that of physical and emotional safety—both regarding the studio itself and the surrounding neighborhood.

CLASSES/SCHEDULE

Class descriptions and schedules offered by a studio will be deciding factors in where you'll enroll your child in dance lessons:

Are classes age-appropriate for your young dancer? Classes geared towards younger dancers generally focus on body awareness, gross motor skill development, listening skills, musicality, and nurturing the creative spirit; typical "genres" of these classes will include ballet, tap, jazz, rhythm, and tumbling.

Can the class(es) be incorporated into your family's overall schedule? For young dancers, class duration ranges from 30-60 minutes per week, with the classes meeting once a week. These classes are generally held on weekday mornings, early weekday afternoons, and/or Saturday mornings.

COST

Cost is a known factor when considering family expenditures. Prices are generally similar for dance studios in the same region, but final prices will be studio-specific. Weigh any differences in cost with location, studio environment, class schedule, and quality of training. A slightly less expensive studio further away might cost the same when adding up the extra travel time and mileage. A studio with higher costs in a safer neighborhood might spare you some stress and worry. As well, a more expensive studio may be justified because of higher quality of dance training and better instructor credentials.

CLASS OBSERVATION

Not all studio facilities are set up for parents to directly observe their child's class. If this is a deal breaker for you, look for studios with either viewing windows or a Closed-Circuit TV (CCTV) in the lobby. CCTV allows you to view the class via live video—usually with no sound—without being a distraction to the teacher or students. Check studio rules—parent observation of classes may either be discouraged or disallowed. Some studios may have observation weeks throughout the dance year for parents to observe their child from within the classroom.

TIPS AND SAFETY REMINDERS FOR THE YOUNGER DANCER

- **Prior to your child's first class**
  - Schedule time to **meet with the teacher** to understand the purpose and structure of the class, what happens during class, and the teacher's expectations. This is a great first step toward developing a rapport and creating a positive experience for your child.
  - Especially important for the younger dancer, unless enrolled in parent-child class (in which you'll participate), **let your child know that you will not be in the room** during the dance lesson, but you'll be right outside.
  - Get your child excited by preparing dance clothes and footwear the night before!
- **Before each class begins,** encourage your child to take **a trip to the restroom.**
- **During your child's class**
  - Like most parents of young dancers, you'll likely stay at the studio to offer encouragement and support for your child. Your presence also gives you the opportunity to develop relationships with other parents, gather information, and actively participate in your child's dance environment.
  - If you can't stay, let the instructor know that your child may need help changing shoes or going to the restroom. It is important that he or she behave appropriately in your absence.
  - Your presence in the studio will be required less as your child grows in age and maturity and becomes more comfortable with the studio staff and fellow dancers.
- **After your child's class**
  - Students should always remain inside the studio until their parents (or designated persons) are there to pick them up. Unless you've given permission to the studio beforehand, **your child should never leave or be allowed to leave the studio with anyone other than you.** Give studio staff the names of persons permitted to leave with your child—for both planned and unexpected situations.

Example of CCTV

Example of Viewing Window

DRESS CODE

When dancers are very young, **acceptable attire** includes comfortable clothing they can move in; dance footwear (e.g., ballet slippers and tap shoes) is recommended but not always required. **Street shoes are not suitable** for dance floors.

As young children grow in dance, they'll be asked to wear more **traditional dance attire.** Coming to class in dance clothing helps younger dancers understand that they're entering a structured setting and gives them the feeling of being a dancer.

The below table serves as a **general guideline** regarding what most dance studios consider traditional attire for young students. As always, be sure to check with the dance studio about any specific requirements.

	Gender	Clothes	Footwear	Hair
For the Younger Dancer Ages 2-5	Girls	Leotard (of any color), pink tights or white socks; ballet skirts and tutus are acceptable	Pink ballet slippers or tap shoes	Hair tied back in ponytail or bun
	Boys	Form-fitting leggings or black shorts, white t-shirt	Black ballet slippers or tap shoes	Short, clean-cut hair that doesn't cover the face and neck

WHAT ARE CONVERTIBLE TIGHTS?

Tights that have an opening in the bottom of the foot, so they can either be worn over the dancer's foot or off the foot at the ankles (as footless tights). Also known as "transition" tights.

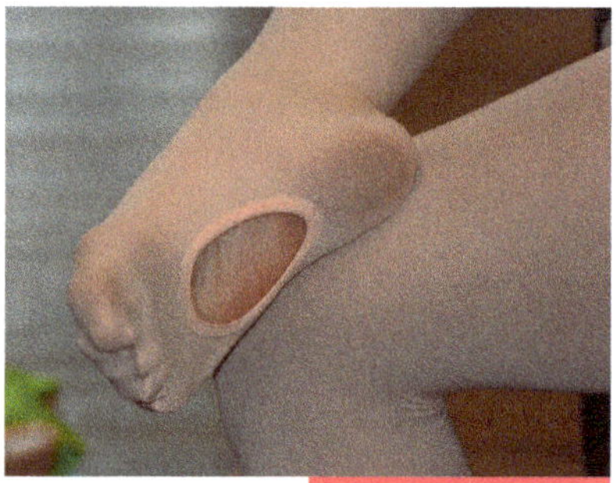

Dance clothing for younger dancers can be purchased online, at brick and mortar stores (e.g., Walmart, Target), at local dance shops, or at your studio (if they sell dancewear).

Dance footwear can be purchased online, at local dance shops, or at your studio (if they sell dance footwear).

NOTES

Photo Credit - JCM Photography

"I dance because I love how it makes me feel. The risks that I take make me stronger and more confident. I have learned from my dance family how to work with others and how to challenge myself to be a better person. Dance will always be a part of who I am and I can't wait to see what the future holds."
-Brooke Brisben, Dancer

Photo Credit - Danielle Trina Photography

© iStock Photo / wwing

THE ANNUAL DANCE RECITAL, FESTIVAL, OR PERFORMANCE SHOWCASE

Featuring routines learned in recreational classes, the **annual recital**[2] is a performance held by a dance studio for the enjoyment of its students and their family and friends. Featuring costumes and choreographies that help display students' skills, **recital is the crescendo of yearlong growth, development, and commitment.**

Recital might be the first time many young dancers perform in front of an audience, so it may be a little nerve-wracking and might even provoke some anxiety. But recitals give students a platform to build their self-confidence and courage by learning to temper fear and stage fright—a valuable skill to develop.

» In addition to a year-end recital, some studios will put on a holiday performance in December. «

[2] For the purposes of this book, "recital" herein will be used to imply a dance "recital," "festival," "spring show," "extravaganza," or "performance showcase."

"It takes time to get a dance right, to create something memorable."

— FRED ASTAIRE

© Can Stock Photo / iqoncept

RECITAL PARTICIPANTS

Each dance studio will make its own determination regarding which routines—and respective participants—will be invited to become part of the recital line-up.

Participation in recital may or may not be mandatory. If not mandatory, students should be able to opt out of one, some, or all classes by filling out a **non-participation form.** This might occur if the child is not available to participate on the recital date, if the child began a recreational dance class late in the dance year and hasn't had enough time to learn the routine, or if the family doesn't want to incur the recital costs. Even if your child is not able to participate in recital, some studios will still require a payment for recital fee and costume expense.

Below is a list of common recital participants:

RECREATIONAL DANCERS

Students enrolled in a studio's recreational dance program are invited to participate in recital. The recital line-up may include a routine for each recreational class or a reduced number of routines by either combining classes (e.g., a single ballet number with students from all levels) or eliminating some classes from the recital altogether. Reducing the number of routines is usually done to best manage the total duration of the recital or to keep overall costs down for families, especially those who have children in multiple classes.

COMPETITIVE DANCERS

If a studio has a competitive dance program, competition group and solo/duet/trio routines may be incorporated into the recital line-up.

SENIOR DANCERS

Graduating seniors may be given the opportunity to perform a solo routine (often self-choreographed) and also special recognition by studio staff.

RECITAL – PROS & CONS

While there are many positive aspects to participating in a recital, there are also drawbacks that should be fairly noted:

ON THE ONE HAND, RECITAL

- Gives dancers the opportunity to **show off** their "moves" in front of family and friends and **experience pride in their well-earned accomplishments** and progress.
- **Inspires children** to continue the art of dancing and performing, opening their eyes to the possibility and pleasure of having the capability to entertain and delight others.
- **Teaches children retention and memorization skills** as they learn dance routines.
- **Encourages teamwork**, as students work toward a common goal.
- **Strengthens bonds between dancers, families, and staff,** forging a stronger sense of camaraderie, pride, and belonging.
- Offers the potential to make **lifelong memories and friendships**.

ON THE OTHER HAND, RECITAL

- Can evoke **anxiety, fear, and discomfort**. For children and adults alike, performing on a stage is a far cry from dancing in the studio. Children might not be prepared for stage lights, the **absence of** teachers (who do I follow?), and a **lack of mirrors** (how do I see myself?). Most importantly, they will be dancing in front of a large audience, which can be quite an intimidating setting for a young child.
- Can be stressful. **A recital is complex; it's time-driven and includes many components.** Before and during the event itself, the recital can be stressful for the studio staff, children, and parents. Quick costume changes (especially when a child's numbers are scheduled close together) can add pressure that must be managed.

> Don't be surprised if your dancer is the best in the studio room and yet, on stage, he or she freezes. As well, if your dancer is shy in the studio room, he or she may just surprise you and light up the stage.

TIPS & HINTS

- Your dance studio may require **all recital fees to be paid in full and a $0 account balance** for the dancer to participate in a recital.
- **Being prepared and organized**—and having the right mindset and attitude—will drastically help to **diffuse stressful situations and tensions** during this time-driven event.
- There can be **a lot of time between your child's dance numbers** as you wait to see him or her shine on stage; sit back and enjoy the full performance.
- If you're volunteering **as a "Stage Parent,"** fulfilling your responsibilities of helping other dancers prepare to go onstage, you may miss your child's recital number(s). If you want to see him or her perform—and you have the flexibility to step away from these responsibilities—keep an eye on the clock as well as the pace of the recital so you can get to the auditorium in time. If needed, find another volunteer to fill your role for the few minutes your child is on stage.
- Recital is an opportunity to **observe what older or more advanced dancers are capable of** and how studio staff work "behind the scenes"—often a good way to gain insight into the studio's training and culture.

"Recitals are a BLAST! There's something exhilarating about being involved in this time-driven event where dancers can show off their hard work and improvement over the dance year! The first few years I felt "lost"—but I still remember the veteran dance moms that gladly helped me find my way. Now that I have the hang of it, it's my pleasure to return the favor and help novice dance moms have a smooth, enjoyable experience!"
-B. Houben

LEADING UP TO RECITAL

Although **each studio will have a unique "formula"** leading up to and during a recital, below are typical steps in the process.

1. PLANNING

A recital can last anywhere from **a single evening to an entire weekend. Preparations begin several months before the actual event** when the studio staff chooses a recital theme, sets a date, books the venue, confirms a photographer and videographer, begins developing routines, and selects costumes. Recital is the result of many months worth of time and effort required to plan and prepare for the big event!

Recitals are typically held **at the end of the dance year**—in May or June—and usually **at a local high school or performing arts center.** The recital date should be communicated to families at the beginning of the dance year and can even be set as early as a year in advance. While the recital date(s) for some studios will vary from year to year, for others, recital is always "Mother's Day weekend," "the Saturday of Father's Day weekend," "the first Thursday in June," or "the second Saturday in June"—year after year.

2. DEVELOPING PROGRAM & MARKETING

The studio will produce and sell a printed recital program, which may include

- **Staff member introductions**
- A chronological **list of the routines (line-up)** with names of respective dancers and choreographers
- Write-ups for **graduating students**
- Company **team highlights**
- **Summer and fall program/schedule information**
- **Advertisements** (space purchased by local businesses)
- **Dancer dedications** (space purchased **to say something special to dance students)**

Sample Recital Dedications
Photo Credit – Danielle Trina Photography

The recital program serves multiple purposes. First and foremost, it gives information about the recital event. It also encourages enrollment in a studio's programs and is a keepsake to remember the special event.

3. LEARNING ROUTINES

Usually **starting in January, during recreational classes**—in addition to technique training—students will learn and rehearse routines to be performed at the year-end recital. For example, young dancers in a Ballet/Tap Combo class will learn a single routine and perform it at recital; students who are taking four recreational dance classes—like Ballet I, Tap II, Jazz II, and Hip Hop I—may learn up to four routines and perform all of them at recital.

Measuring for Recital

4. PARTICIPATING IN COSTUME MEASURING WEEK

Stay informed about the when and where of **"Measuring Week"**—mark it on your calendar!

The studio will select and order recital costumes, often as early as November of the current dance year. Before the order goes out, the studio will plan days for student measurements to be taken by either studio staff or dance moms so that the correct sizes are ordered. Children will likely grow throughout the year, so measurements should allow room for growth.

Measurements and correct sizing should be confirmed when the costumes arrive at the studio. If there is an issue with your child's costume, there's **no need to panic** as there are steps you can take to correct the situation. Costumes can be returned, if time allows, or can alternatively be tailored or swapped with other dancers if they also have a sizing issue.

5. TAKING RECITAL PICTURES

At some point before recital, most dance studios schedule recital **Picture Day(s)** where a local, professional photographer takes group pictures of each recreational dance class in costume. Pictures are **typically taken at the studio**, but photo sessions may also be held at the recital hall or at a suitable outdoor location.

Although not mandatory, all dancers participating in the recital are requested to be present for Picture Day(s) so the studio and other students have a picture of the entire class. **Bring all costumes, footwear, tights, and accessories** that will be worn during the recital; **make sure personal jewelry and nail polish are removed.**

If your child cannot attend the photo session, let studio staff know ahead of time so they aren't waiting for someone who won't be showing up.

If your child *does* attend, ***arrive at the specified time and ensure your child is prepared—costume, hair, and makeup included.*** Your studio may request a specific recital hairstyle to be worn for pictures (e.g., a bun). For a clean look, secure hair with bobby pins and a hairnet; tame flyaway strands with gel, and smooth hair with hairspray. Makeup may not be required for younger dancers, but know that a little bit of blush and lip gloss can enhance your child's look under the harsh lights.

Stock Images: © Can Stock Photo / Pixart

On Picture Day(s), you can generally expect

- **Regular classes will not be scheduled.**
- **A detailed schedule will be sent** to you beforehand for planning purposes.
- The studio will have **ordered and received recital costumes** that should already be fitted for your child.
- **Dressing rooms** will be available for dancers who require costume changes. If pictures are taken at the dance studio, studio rooms are typically converted into dressing rooms.
- **Parents will not be allowed in the photo studio** with their children. This arrangement is best for time-management and the safety of the students and photographic equipment. Children should know ahead of time so they won't be surprised when their parents don't accompany them.
- **Ordering recital pictures should be optional.** If you do wish to purchase photos, the studio will offer order forms; options and prices will vary. Photographs are often available within a few weeks. Professional **photographers may offer package deals** (the more pictures ordered, the lower the price per picture).

RECITAL PICTURE DAYS

Recital class pictures will be taken May 16-19.
These will take place at the studio. On these days, there will not be regular classes, just photos. Each class will run through their dance in their costume on this day.

DETAILED PICTURE SCHEDULE WILL BE OUT BY APRIL 18TH! WE HAVE A NEW PHOTOGRAPHER THAT WE THINK ALL OF YOU WILL LOVE.

All pictures will be available for digital download sent to your email
Package A: $15.00-1 class picture
Package B: $30.00-1 class picture and 2 individual poses
Package C: $50.00-All class pictures (for 1 dancer) and 2 poses in each

Sample picture recital information provided by a dance studio

6. BUYING TICKETS, FLOWERS, AND RECITAL GIFTS

Order **recital tickets** online or at your studio when they become available. Check to see if tickets include assigned or open seating.

Bestowing flowers upon dancers is customary at the end of a recital performance. As a convenience, many studios will sell bouquets to their dance families either by

- Taking orders and payment in advance and bringing the bouquets to the recital venue for pickup.
- Selling bouquets at the recital venue.

If your studio doesn't sell flowers, you can stop by your local grocery store or florist to pick up a bouquet.

Giving **recital gifts** to studio staff (owner(s), instructors, choreographers), parents, or dancers is often customary at recital. Some studios will set a maximum price for recital gifts (e.g., $20). Inquire with your studio to learn more about this tradition.

Tututix provides an online system used by many dance studios for selling recital tickets.
tututix.com

7. PARTICIPATING IN RECITAL WEEK

Rehearsals usually take place over several days during the week leading up to the recital event. Since rehearsals are an essential component in readying dancers and routines, they're often mandatory for all participants. **Recital week** may include a technical rehearsal and/or a dress rehearsal.

- **Technical Rehearsal:** This is intended to work out all details of music, spacing, lighting, sequencing, props, etc. Typically, the dancers will wear something comfortable (e.g., street clothing or dancewear) with no hair and makeup requirements.
- **Dress Rehearsal:** Known also as a "mock" or "full-dress rehearsal," this is the final rehearsal before the recital performance. Dancers perform numbers in full makeup, hairdo, and costume (with props, if utilized) so that choreographers and staff members can assess performance readiness and tweak routines as appropriate. Although each studio will schedule recital weeks differently, below is a **real-world example of the week leading up to and including the final recital:**

Tuesday	Wednesday	Thursday	Friday	Saturday
Technical Rehearsal for Friday and Saturday shows	Dress Rehearsal for Friday shows	Dress Rehearsal for Saturday shows	Recital	Recital
3:30-8:30PM	3:30-8:30PM	3:30-8:30PM	6:30-8:30PM	6:30-8:30PM

KEEP IN MIND...

- During Recital Week, **all dance classes may be canceled**.
- Studio staff will let you know if there are **volunteer opportunities** to support Recital Week; if they forget and you're interested, feel free to ask about how to get involved.
- Recital Week can be **hectic and time-consuming.** As far in advance as possible, update your family's calendar with dance commitments, and try not to plan anything else during the week. Make sure to review and understand all studio communications so that you can be best prepared.
- During rehearsals, both dancers and parents should take advantage of the downtime in between numbers. If the studio allows it, **bring water, snacks, and activities (coloring books, games, etc.)** to keep your child hydrated, fueled, and occupied. Don't bring food or drinks that can stain costumes or other dance items.
- Check with studio staff to understand the **rules about taking pictures and videos** during rehearsals (some studios will allow this, others will not). If allowed, this is a great time to capture memories prior to the actual recital event during which photography and videography is generally prohibited.
- **Label all your child's belongings** by writing his or her name with a permanent marker on bags or tags including costumes, tights, accessories, etc.

The prop trailer arrives at the recital venue!

A WORD OF ADVICE ABOUT MAKEUP

Given the harshness of stage lights and the distance between the stage and the audience, **makeup is essential for livening up a dancer's face.** Professional actors and dancers know very well that "performance makeup" is actually different—more colorful and plentiful—than an everyday application of makeup. Under bright stage lights, faces without makeup can seem washed-out and sickly, even when they appear (and are!) perfectly healthy and radiant when illuminated by more natural light. Performance makeup also **helps draw more attention to facial expressions and enhances the overall look** of costuming.

Your studio may specify the **colors and brand of makeup** to be worn. They may also offer makeup sessions or **online videos to demonstrate how to apply makeup.**

It may be awkward for younger dancers and their parents to be confronted with the idea of stage makeup—it's such a grownup thing to do! In most cases, it will be acceptable to your studio for younger dancers to apply a lesser amount of stage makeup.

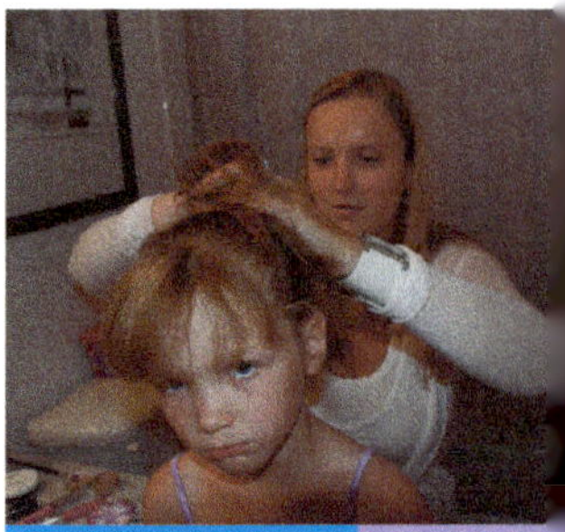

Hair and makeup on little ones can be a challenge!

For **minimal makeup**, consider

- A few strokes of mascara
- A bit of blush to highlight the cheekbones
- A swipe of lip gloss to color the mouth

For a more complete application of **stage makeup**, add

- Foundation that matches the dancer's skin tone
- Eyeliner, eyeshadow, and mascara and/or false eyelashes
- Lip primer, lip liner, and lipstick

MAKE UP DOS AND DON'TS

- **DON'T** try makeup on for the first time on the day of recital. Some children may have allergic reactions, so it's wise to work this out in advance of the event. If your child is sensitive to makeup, consider organic or natural products.
- **DO** apply makeup before your child is dressed to avoid makeup products from dripping or dropping on costumes.
- **DO** have your child wear a cap or cover-up if you apply make after the costume is on.
- **DON'T** apply overly creative or dramatic makeup. Too much makeup is just as bad as none.
- **DO** use primers to prevent smudging lipstick and foundation.

REMOVING MAKEUP

Purchase over the counter products to remove eye and facial makeup, or you might want to consider a more natural option with less chemicals and lower overall cost, especially for younger children. **Conservativedancewear.blogspot.com** has posted a helpful blog (March 2014) about taking a more natural route:

- Remove makeup by patting the face with a cotton round that's been infused with a few drops of extra-virgin olive oil or almond oil, then rinsing the face with warm water.
- Alternatively, try witch hazel as a stand-alone product or mixed with a bit of olive oil, applied and washed off in the same way.

"I tell the girls, 'If you're under the age of ten, someone must help you put on lipstick.' Otherwise mistakes with lipstick are very hard to correct, especially during a time-driven event, such as recital." -Stacy Brisben, Stage Mom

PARENT PARTICIPATION

Support for recital includes getting your child to rehearsals and photo sessions, making sure costumes are ready, setting hair and makeup, and being present at recital where you'll watch your child perform on stage. But why not take it a step further? Remember, the studio might ask for **volunteers,** or you can proactively inquire about volunteer opportunities. Volunteering enables you to both support your child and the studio staff in preparation for, during, and after the recital event.

Although each dance studio will have its own needs and volunteer positions, here are a few examples of real-life recital roles for both moms and dads, with respective responsibilities:

THE STAGE PARENT/ROOM PARENT

To most effectively manage dancers and the associated activity, many studios will assign one or more stage parents whose responsibilities may include

- Ensuring dancers are stage-ready (e.g., costume changes, hair, and makeup).
- Escorting ("running") dance groups to and from the stage and dressing room (before and after their numbers are performed).
- Being available to dancers in the dressing room for any reason.

THE PROP DAD

Although moms can also fulfill this role, it's typically dance dads who **assist in transporting props to and from the recital venue as well as placing and removing props on stage** when they are used in performances.

THE GREETER/USHER

Greets guests, collects their tickets, and directs them to their seats in the auditorium.

THE CASHIER

Sells tickets, programs, and concessions during the recital event.

"Prop dads are integral to the success of recitals and competition events. Taking on this role allows fathers to get involved in their child's dance experience and gain appreciation of studio staff and dance families alike."
-B. Houben

RECITAL READINESS CHECKLIST

Use the following list as a reference to ensure you and your dancer are ready for recital:

- ☐ **Purchase recital tickets** for family and friends. In some cases, tickets can sell out quickly, so make sure you purchase tickets in a timely manner.
- ☐ If available, **submit a dedication to your child in the recital program**; with verbiage and a picture, this is an opportunity to express your love and pride.
- ☐ Confirm that **you've received all your child's costumes and accessories** and that they are fitted for size.
- ☐ **Practice applying makeup and preparing the recital hairstyle** to work out any kinks before the event.
- ☐ **Label all your dancer's belongings** (especially dance shoes and even bows and tights) with his or her name or initials.
- ☐ Review the "Supply Packing Checklist" on page 105 to **ensure you arrive with everything your child needs** to perform; pack items in a duffel bag and makeup bag.
- ☐ **Pack water and healthy snacks** for staying fueled and hydrated.
  - — Consider packing nut-free items to be considerate of those with allergies.
  - — Avoid drinks and foods that can discolor costumes.
- ☐ Pack something that may **help your dancer stay occupied between his or her numbers** (coloring books and crayons, games, cards, etc.).
- ☐ Buy or make a **recital gift** for studio staff, parents, and/or dancers.
- ☐ **Familiarize yourself with the recital schedule** and your dancer's **"call time"** (the time he or she is due at the venue).
- ☐ **Buy flowers**, if you like; awarding dancers with a bouquet of flowers is a sweet and customary tradition.

Recital Gift

Bouquets of flowers sold by the dance studio

KEEP IN MIND…

- **Arriving on time and being well-prepared**—informed and organized with all essential supplies—will significantly reduce stress and ensure a more enjoyable experience.
- Come to the event with your child already **in costume**, with **completed hairdo and makeup**.
- Have your child consume a healthy meal prior to arrival.
- **Don't bring colorful foods, nail-polish, or glitter** that can stain or damage costumes in any way.
- **Refrain from bringing along valuables** or jewelry that can get lost or caught on costumes.
- Pack an **oversized shirt or cover-up** (button-up, not over-the-head, so as not to mess with hair and makeup) to protect your child's costumes and keep him or her warm between performances.
- **Only allow your dancer to wear costumes at dress rehearsals and at the actual recital to** minimize risk of damage.
- Keep costumes in good condition. You can still **make good use of costumes after recital**—sell them, give them away, or have your child use them for dressing up (e.g., Halloween).
- **Plan to stay for the finale**—this is usually required for all dancers and a lot of fun to see!

Recital builds bonds among dance students!

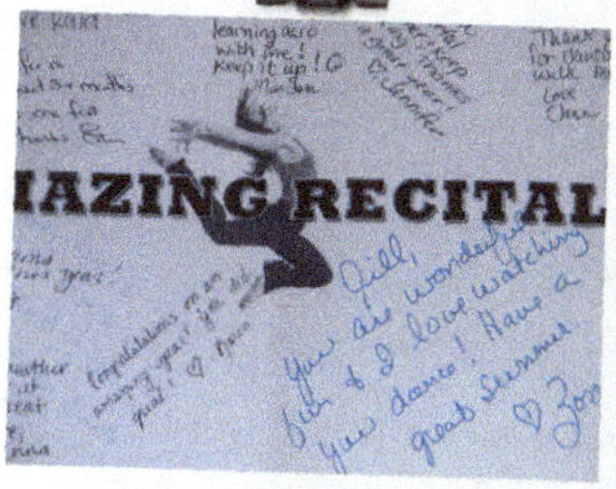

Thank you note from studio staff

SEVEN STAGES OF RECITAL

Although each recital will have its own cadence, below is a list of common stages:

STAGE 1: DANCERS ARRIVE AT THE VENUE AND BEGIN PREPARATIONS IN THE DRESSING ROOM TO GET STAGE-READY.

Your child will be given **"call time"** and asked to **arrive well before the recital start time** to prepare. This might even mean showing up two hours before show time. Dancers (especially young ones) are encouraged to arrive dressed for their first number with their hair and makeup ready to minimize the flurry of activity in the dressing rooms and to reduce last-minute confusion and stress.

Upon arrival to the recital venue, depending upon your studio, you'll **either bring your child to the designated dressing room or to a designated check-in area** to be greeted by a stage parent, staff member, or older dancer who will escort him or her to the dressing room. Once in the dressing room, your child will find a place for his or her belongings and prepare for the show. During the recital, dancers typically remain in the dressing areas in between dance numbers and until the recital is over.

Dressing rooms can get hectic. To most effectively manage dancers and all the behind-the-scenes activity, as mentioned above, many studios only allow assigned **stage parents, staff, and/or older dancers** in the dressing rooms who carry out the responsibilities that, as a mom or dad, you'd expect to do (e.g., costume changes, hair, and makeup). If you are in this situation, handing over control and putting trust in others might be challenging to experience. (If possible, inquire about becoming a stage parent yourself.) On the other hand, it can be a time for you to relax and simply enjoy the show!

Girls' and boys' dressing rooms should be designated and separate. (In some cases, younger dancers may also be separated from older dancers.) Since boys are often the minority, it's important to note that a separate dressing room for them is not always available. Your son may, therefore, need to either change in the restroom or be stage-ready before arrival. The arrangement isn't ideal, but it is doable since boys' costumes and preparation activities are far fewer than girls'. Stage dads, dance dads, or older male dancers can assist younger boys who might need help in getting ready. **For moms, it's best to stay out of the boys' dressing room**—your child may like you there, but your presence can make other boys and their parents uncomfortable.

A dressing room can be **stressful and hectic,** but it can also be **an oasis in which dancers can rest and relax** between numbers. Dancers usually bring a **blanket** to designate their "spot," upon which they'll get stage ready or lie down to rest during downtime. It's also normal to see dancers who are frantically getting their hair ready and putting on costumes, makeup, and accessories for the first or subsequent dance performance(s)—as well as dancers who are chatting, eating snacks, playing games, watching a movie on a mobile device, or coloring.

Expect that most **dance parents and older dancers will be extremely helpful** during recital. People understand that the success of a **recital is a group effort.** Times like these strengthen feelings that embody the "dance family" culture.

STAGE 2: AUDIENCE MEMBERS ARRIVE AND ARE SEATED.
Seating may be **assigned or open.** If you did not **purchase tickets in advance,** there should be an opportunity to **purchase them at the venue,** if the seats haven't been sold out.

STAGE 3: ACT 1. THE RECITAL BEGINS; SEVERAL NUMBERS ARE PERFORMED.
For each dance number, an assigned **staff member, stage parent, or volunteer will escort the group of dancers** from the dressing room to backstage where they'll await their performance. **Grab your seat** in the auditorium and cheer your dancer on! Remember that **personal photography and videography are generally prohibited** during the performance (flashes can distract or upset the dancers onstage). Studios usually hire a photographer and/or videographer to capture images and videos for purchase after the recital.

After **each number is performed, dancers will head back to the dressing area.** If they have additional numbers, dancers will prepare for their next routine. Otherwise, dancers typically remain in costume until the finale. The performance continues until intermission.

Theater Etiquette – TIPS

- Turn **cell phones off** or set on vibrate.
- **Do not eat or drink** in the auditorium.
- If talking is necessary, **keep the volume low.**
- **Do not take pictures** which can distract the dancers on stage.
- **If you need to enter or leave the auditorium during performance, do this in between numbers** so as not to disrupt other audience members whose favorite dancer might just be on stage!

NOT FOLLOWING COMMON SENSE ETIQUETTE CAN UPSET AUDIENCE MEMBERS WHO WISH TO ENJOY THE PERFORMANCE. THIS CAN CARRY OVER TO INTERPERSONAL RELATIONSHIPS WITH PARENTS AT THE STUDIO!

STAGE 4: IT'S TIME FOR INTERMISSION.
A recital intermission usually lasts **about 10-15 minutes.** Often a **concession stand** is set up where audience members can buy food, snacks, and drinks (sometimes these are free; if not, proceeds from sales typically support the studio). Take advantage of this time to **grab a bite, use the restroom, stretch your legs,** and **mingle** with other audience members. Depending on the studio rules and procedures, you may or may not see your child during intermission (he or she may be required to remain in the dressing room until after the finale).

The scene of a recital dressing room.

In the wings, backstage.

STAGE 5: ACT 2. THE RECITAL RESUMES.

After intermission, the **recital performance continues** with the remaining numbers.

STAGE 6: THE FINALE HAPPENS, FEATURING ALL RECITAL DANCERS.

All students are encouraged to participate in a **closing ceremony** for recognition and applause. This phase of a recital can include more choreography (dances) or just a chance for the children to take a bow. It is an opportunity to see your child for (at least) a second time on stage. **Graduating seniors** may be given a special moment of acknowledgment. The finale is a great time to **take personal pictures and videos** (usually allowed at this stage of the event).

STAGE 7: DANCERS RETURN TO THE DRESSING ROOM.

Dancers go back to the dressing room, pack their belongings, and emerge to **reunite with their families and friends.** Since there are many people at a recital, make sure you tell your child ahead of time where you're going to meet him or her after the finale. Although each studio has their own "system," most will have stage parents, staff members, or older dancers bring students from the dressing areas to greet their parents. Give them a big **hug** and **congratulate** them! If you purchased **flowers,** now is the time to bestow them upon your dancer.

ANNUAL DANCE COSTS FOR THE YOUNGER DANCER

For planning and budgeting, it's important to be aware of expenses related to dance. Consider the following scenario within a **single dance year (excluding summer months):** one **4-year old child** taking **one dance class (Ballet/Tap)** and **participating in recital.**

Please note that **THESE COSTS ARE ROUGH ESTIMATES** and may not include all incidental costs. Costs **across regions** and dance studios will vary. Regarding dancewear and footwear, costs will similarly vary based on quality and where they are purchased. Keep in mind that **each year, costs may increase.**

Sample (not actual) **annual costs for a 4-year old dancer for explanatory purposes**		
Item	**Description**	**Expense**
RECREATIONAL DANCE COSTS		
Registration Fee	Due upon registration for recreational classes	$25
Combo (Ballet/Tap) Class	Nine months at $35 per month for a single 30-minute class per week	$315
Dancewear	One leotard ($15), (1) ballet tights ($15)	$30
Footwear	Ballet slippers ($25), tap shoes ($30)	$55
Annual Recreational Total Cost		$425
RECITAL COSTS		
Recital Fee	Due upon commitment to participate in recital	$65
Recital Costume	One costume, tights, and accessories	$100
Recital Tickets	Five tickets for family members and friends at $15 per ticket	$75
Recital Program	One program book	$10
Recital Pictures	One class picture	$15
Recital Gift	One gift	$20
Recital Total Cost		$285

Payment methods (cash, check, or auto-payment) and due dates differ across studios. Late fees can apply, so it's important to clarify the studio policy during enrollment.

Photo Credit - JCM Photography

Photo Credit - Danielle Trina Photography

DANCER'S 8

"5, 6, 7, 8" With Dance, Everything is in an 8-Count.

SPECIFIC TO THE EVOLVING DANCER (6+ YEARS OLD)

This section is geared toward committed (competitive or performance-based) dancers.

Bitten by the Dance Bug defines an **"evolving dancer"** as either **the child who has already been through beginner dance classes** or the **older child who has decided he or she would like to start taking dance lessons.** For each scenario, it's time to engage in intermediary and advanced classes that offer higher training levels and a greater variety of dance genres.

It's never too late to start taking recreational dance classes. However, in pursuit of a dance career—excluding the exceptions—the norm will require that a student start training (latest) by his or her early teens, and that's assuming a natural affinity for dance. Ballet and pointe training should start at an early age so that the ballet dancer can capture the correct look for professional ballet.

> ***"I feel like going to class every morning is so humbling. You're always working to improve, and you're always being critiqued on your next performance. It's not about what you've done. There's always room to grow."***
>
> — MISTY COPELAND

SELECTING THE IDEAL DANCE STUDIO

Below are overarching factors for parents of evolving dancers when choosing a dance studio for their child:

CLASSES/SCHEDULE

For the evolving dancer, while it is certainly a matter of **transitioning through levels and to new dance genres,** it is also sometimes a matter of **transitioning from one dance studio to another**. Even if you're perfectly satisfied with the current studio, it might not offer classes that are convenient or training that is focused in a specific dance genre (e.g., ballet or hip hop) that your child is interested in. Additionally, it might not be as competitive as you and your child may desire. In whichever studio you enroll, the **staff should be available to identify appropriate classes and levels** for your child.

As commitment increases, your dancer's schedule will require additional student and family planning. For evolving dancers, each class duration typically ranges from 60-90 minutes per week on weekdays (after-school hours) or Saturday mornings. For example, Ballet I may be scheduled each Monday from 4:00PM to 5:00PM. The number of classes (hours) will naturally increase.

QUALITY OF DANCE INSTRUCTION

A continued investment in dance training means that the **quality of dance instructors** should be more closely evaluated—especially important for students who have potential, appear ready to increase their commitment, and have an interest in a dance future. Quality training entails the **study of technique** that helps dancers reach certain performance levels by mastering proper body alignment, building strength and flexibility, and minimizing injuries. Make time to seek out and **read instructor biographies and studio credentials** (all of which should be available on the studio's website). Also talk with other parents and dancers about their personal evaluation of the instructors.

FAMILIARITY

An often-used term within dance studios is "**dance family.**" This term becomes relevant as you and your child's commitment to dance grows. Many clients consider studio staff and fellow dance parents and dancers their "family" because of the **time spent together,** their **shared goals,** and their **dependence upon each other.** Within the setting of a dance studio, there's rich potential for both children and parents to make solid and long-lasting friendships. Many families will choose to remain at their studio with their "family" rather than seek alternatives.

LOCATION

As your child participates in more dance classes, you'll likely be traveling to the dance studio multiple times a week. The proximity of the dance studio to your home, school, office, and family members becomes even more relevant. As you familiarize yourself with other dance families, consider carpooling to reduce the demands and costs of commuting. And again, above all, the safety of the studio and its location must reign as a primary factor.

COST

As the amount of dance classes increases, cost will continue to be a consideration. Prices are generally similar for studios in the same region, but final prices will be studio-specific. Weigh any differences in cost with location, schedule, and quality of training. Also, as mentioned in the **Expenses and Payments section on page 6**, learn about any discounts that might be available to your situation.

NOTES

TIPS AND SAFETY REMINDERS

- Once enrolled, your child should always arrive on time and in the appropriate attire for class. **Arriving late or unprepared is both disrespectful and distracting,** not only for the instructor, but for other students who want to gain the most out of their time in studio.
- If your child has more than one class per day, these classes may run back-to-back with no break in between. Especially in such cases, you'll want to **make sure your dancer is properly hydrated and fed** before his or her first lesson begins. You can always pack small snacks (or buy snacks if they're sold at the studio) since instructors may allow students to grab a quick bite in between classes. Have your dancer **pack a bottle of water;** staying hydrated is especially important since water is significant for healthfully regulating bodily functions and keeping both the brain and body alert.
- Some studios actively discourage parents of older (and self-sufficient) dancers from staying in the studio during their child's classes. Learning without parental supervision is typically less stressful for dance students, and not having parents around physically gives staff and dancers more room to function.
- Students should stay inside the studio until you arrive. Unless you've given permission to the studio beforehand, **your child should never leave or be allowed to leave the studio with anyone other than you.** Give studio staff the names of persons who have your permission to leave with your child—for both planned and unexpected situations.

© Can Stock Photo / Antonio_Diaz

© Can Stock Photo / dotshock

INCREASINGLY IMPORTANT–TECHNIQUE

As lovely young dancers grow and mature, they will **transition into a more serious study of proper technique, poise, discipline, and artistic development of dance.**

BALLET IS THE FOUNDATION OF DANCE!

Ballet is considered the most difficult of all dance forms. It is unique because the dancer is always working turned out. **"Turnout" is the ability to rotate the legs outward from the hips,** allowing the knee to align correctly over the foot. This rotation is supported by proper placement of the knees, feet, all adjoining muscles from the hips and abdomen down through the feet—and the strength to hold the rotation. That **rotation is fundamental to ballet.** Each dancer has a natural range of turnout that can be enhanced—to some degree—through ballet training.

While the art of ballet is universally commended and appreciated for its elements of grace and beauty, it also **demands considerable strength and a very disciplined control of the entire body.** The amount of time, energy, and strength needed to master this form of dance are often underestimated by those who are unaware of ballet's techniques. The **ballet "look"** is completed by very specific use of the head, neck, arms, hands, and upper body; what looks effortless is always the result of countless of hours of practice.

A beautifully pointed foot, a high passé, a clean pirouette, and the line of a correctly executed arabesque result from a close study of ballet. It should come as little surprise, therefore, that **proper ballet technique is the basic foundation of most other forms of dance, including jazz, lyrical, and contemporary.**

In the beginning of your child's dance training, it's important to **be aware of how vital ballet technique is to your dancer's growth,** development, potential—and, consequently, why quality training is of the essence to enable perfect body alignment and placement, build strength and flexibility, and prevent injuries. Serious dancers should thoroughly research dance programs and instructors to ensure they receive high-quality training.

Apart from quality, ballet is also a matter of taste. There are a **variety of methods** to choose from—Cecchetti, Royal Academy of Dance, Vaganova, Balanchine, etc.—and one style may appeal to your dancer more than another. These methods differ in technique and style; however, any one of these methods, when properly done, can enable a dancer to develop clean technique.

COMMON BALLET EXERCISES INCLUDE:

Barre Work—exercises to warm up the body and build the technique needed to work in center floor and across the floor. The barre is a handrail providing support.

Center Floor Work—Steps executed center floor in repetition and/or combinations of varying length in the center of the room.

Across the Floor Work-Steps executed in repetition and/or combinations of varying length as dancers move across the floor. This is sometimes known as "diagonals."

© Can Stock Photo / Antonio_Diaz

KEEP IN MIND…

- **The older a child becomes, the more difficult it is to correct improper technique,** possibly resulting in a missed opportunity that may never be available to your child again.
- **Ballet terms are often taught in French;** some terms your child will learn include *chaînés, chassé, demi-plié,* and *relevé.*
- Dancers are often encouraged to **keep a journal** with choreography, corrections, and coaching tips.
- To emphasize the importance of training and make the most of it, most dance studios with a **competitive or pre-professional dance program will require several hours of ballet per week.**

WHAT IS YAGP?

Youth America Grand Prix (YAGP) is a prestigious, annual, world-wide ballet competition.

For an abundance of information, go to www.yagp.org or check out Ballet Talk for Dancers at www.dancers.invisionzone.com.

APRIL 29

INTERNATIONAL DANCE DAY

JULY (LAST SATURDAY)

NATIONAL DANCE DAY

CLASSES AND GENRES

As your dancer progresses in the art of recreational dance and enrolls in more classes, you will, in turn, be exposed to new levels of knowledge and understanding. "Genres" are the different styles of dance. Here is a list of common genres with common class descriptions:

Acro/Tumbling	Classical dance combined with tumbling and acrobatic techniques such as walkovers, handsprings and aerials.
Ballet	A classical form of dance with exercises geared towards balance, alignment, body placement, flexibility, and strength to create an art form through precise movements, steps, and gestures. Classes include traditional barre, center, and across the floor work.
Contemporary	An expressive movement that combines ballet, jazz, lyrical, and modern dance elements that can be performed to any type of music. This form of dance is typically performed by more experienced dancers who illustrate the harmony of mind and body through fluid dance movements.
Hip Hop	A "combo" class of high energy "street" dance that is characterized by breaking, popping, and locking movements.
Jazz	A high-energy dance form that utilizes up-tempo music and requires proper dance techniques, including turns and jumps; incorporates elements of ballet, lyrical, and modern dance.
Lyrical	A "combo" class of ballet and jazz that is characterized by flowing, fluid movements that are meant to express emotions; it is performed to music with lyrics.
Modern	Use of modern dance elements including balance, control, and extension movements.
Musical Theater	A "combo class" with Broadway and/or theatre dance styles that offers a combination of jazz, modern, and ballet genres; dances are often set to songs from Broadway shows. This style employs both dance and acting abilities. Musical Theater often includes lip-synching.
Pom	A combination of cheerleading and dancing techniques using pom-poms.
Tap	A form of dance characterized by rhythmical patterns and sounds created by the feet clad in specific shoes that have metal plates at the toe and heel.
Pointe	An advanced form of ballet training in pointe shoes.
Turns, Jumps and Tricks	A class focused specifically on improving technique, specifically through the practice of turns, leaps, and other dance "tricks."
Strength and Flexibility	A class focused on stretching exercises meant to enhance muscle flexibility, the joints' range of motion, technique, and body lines, as well as to strengthen muscles. When conducted properly, these exercises can drastically reduce the risk for injury.

Combinations (or **"combos,"** as they are typically called) are an **integral part of a dancer's day-to-day training.** A combo is basically a **series of dance steps linked together in a sequence and performed to music.** Combos are **taught by a lead-by-example method:** the teacher demonstrates the steps and dancers execute them. Musical theater, hip hop, and lyrical classes are all "combo-based," therefore placing heavy emphasis on stylization and choreography. The **purpose of combos is to develop memorization and choreography skills and to prepare dancers for the stage** where they'll perform longer pieces that can be interpreted as a series of combos.

DRESS CODE

In recreational dance classes, there is an **appropriate attire for each genre.** Teachers generally prefer dancers to wear form-fitting clothes in order to better discern body alignment and movement. There is also the expectation that the **dancer's hair be prepared according to the dance genre** (generally pulled back from the face and off the neck so that it looks polished and doesn't become annoying or distracting). The table below can serve as a **general guideline.** As always, be sure to check with your dance studio about their specific requirements.

DANCE TYPE	CLOTHES	FOOTWEAR	HAIR
Acro	Form-fitting leggings or shorts with a sports bra or form-fitting top	Jazz shoes or barefoot	Bun or ponytail
Ballet (Girls)	Black leotard, pink tights	Pink ballet slippers	Longer hair in a bun, short hair pulled off face with a headband or barrettes, no bangs
Pointe (Girls)	Black leotard, pink tights	Pointe shoes	Longer hair in a bun, short hair pulled off face with a headband or barrettes, no bangs
Ballet (Boys)	Black dance pants, shorts, or tights; solid, form-fitting white t-shirt	Black ballet slippers with white socks	Clean-cut, off the face and neck
Hip Hop	Sweatpants or loose-fitting athletic pants that are easy to move in, tank top or t-shirt	Athletic sneakers with non-black soles (black soles can leave marks on the floor)	Ponytail or unbound
Jazz	Form-fitting leggings or shorts with sports bra or form-fitting top	Jazz shoes or barefoot	Longer hair in a bun, short hair pulled off face with a headband or barrettes
Tap	Form-fitting leggings or shorts with sports bra or form-fitting top	Tap shoes	Longer hair in a bun or ponytail, short hair pulled off face with a headband or barrettes
Musical Theater	Leotard, jazz pants or dance shorts with a camisole	Jazz shoes, character shoes (usually for more advanced dancers)	Longer hair in a bun, short hair pulled off face with a headband or barrettes
Lyrical	Solid-colored leotard, form-fitting leggings or shorts with sports bra or form-fitting top	Dance paws, half-sole dance shoes, socks, or barefoot	Longer hair in a bun or ponytail; for short hair, pulled off face with a headband or barrettes. Unbound hair is sometimes acceptable
Modern/ Contemporary	Solid colored leotard, form-fitting leggings or shorts with sports bra or form-fitting top	Dance paw shoes, half-sole dance shoes, socks, or barefoot	Longer hair in a bun or ponytail; for short hair, pulled off face with a headband or barrettes. Unbound hair is sometimes acceptable
Pom	Form-fitting leggings or shorts with sports bra or form-fitting top	Jazz shoes	Pulled neatly off the face in a bun or ponytail

FOR FEMALE DANCERS

When a ballet class is directly followed by another recreational class and there's limited time to change—wear a leotard with convertible tights. She can just throw on shorts, pull the convertible tights off her feet, put on the appropriate footwear, and go!

HOW DRESS CODE CAN DIFFER BETWEEN STUDIOS

Here are some examples of how the dress code for recreational classes can vary from studio to studio:

- Each ballet level wears a different color leotard with pink tights (e.g., Ballet 5 wears a black leotard, Ballet 4 wears a red leotard, Ballet 3 wears a blue leotard, etc.).
- Two-piece outfits are only allowed on certain days of the week or not at all.
- Only the color black can be worn in studio for all recreational classes.

Photo Credit - JCM Photography

DANCE FOOTWEAR

As noted in the dress code table on the previous page, each dance genre's outfit demands appropriate footwear. Below are footwear types for a variety of dance genres (there are many more products in the market than shown).

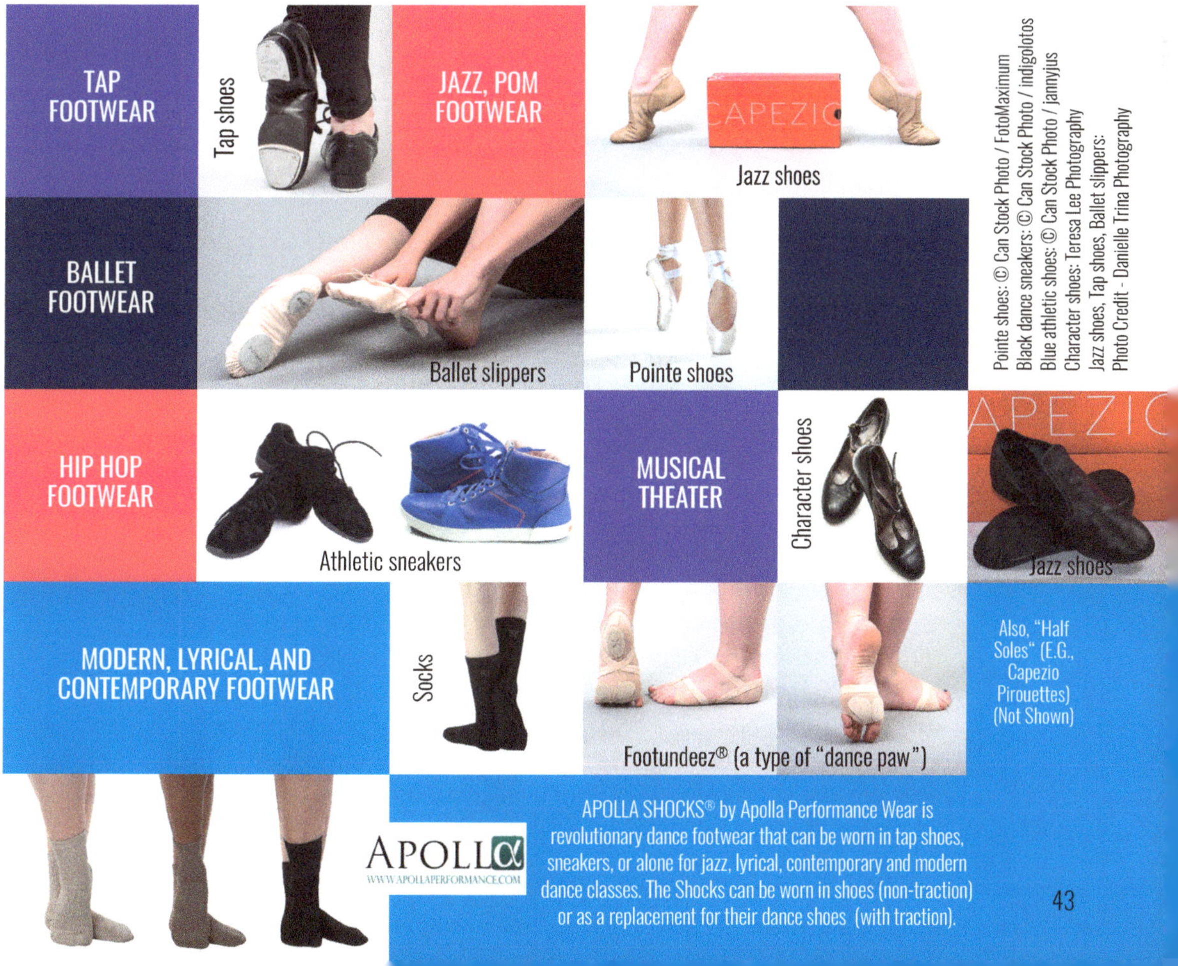

Pointe shoes: © Can Stock Photo / FotoMaximum
Black dance sneakers: © Can Stock Photo / indigolotos
Blue athletic shoes: © Can Stock Photo / jannyjus
Character shoes: Teresa Lee Photography
Jazz shoes, Tap shoes, Ballet slippers:
Photo Credit - Danielle Trina Photography

Photo credit - Canela Photography

ALL-NATURAL REFRESHING FOOT SPRITZ
Cools, deodorizes and soothes tired feet. Specially formulated for dancers!
www.getfreshified.com

TRICKS OF THE TRADE—FOOTWEAR ODOR PREVENTION & CONTROL

- Wear clean socks with shoes when possible.
- Use insoles as appropriate (e.g., Odor-Eaters®).
- Put baking soda in the shoes daily, after class.
- Use sprays (like Freshify™, Odor-Eaters® Stink Stoppers™, Sweet Feet™, Funkaway™, Sof Sole® Fresh Fogger), and oils (e.g., Kids Safe® Odor Zapper).
- Put shoes in a bag with fresheners (e.g., sneaker balls)
- Put shoes in Ziploc® bag with baking soda in them and put them in the freezer overnight. (Hot Tip!)

OR, REPLACE THE FOOTWEAR—IT MIGHT JUST BE THAT TIME!

Credit: Sweet Feet LLC | www.sweetfeetllc.com

FOOTWEAR TIPS & HINTS

- **Dance shoes that don't fit properly or don't provide the proper support can hamper training and performance results.**
- For dance **students at lower class levels, seek approval from the instructor regarding shoe purchases** to ensure proper fitting *before* they're worn in case you need to return them to the store or change the size or style.
- **Shoes vary in quality and price**, so learn to differentiate when a high-quality shoe is worth the cost.
- **Be careful when ordering shoes online;** make sure to reference a conversion chart between street shoe size and dance shoe size. Sometimes design and form can influence what size your child actually needs, too. Alternatively, whenever possible, visit a local shop and get shoes fitted before ordering them online so that you know exactly which size is needed.
- **Ordering pointe shoes online can be risky** because both the size and the shape of the foot must be considered. Visit a local professional pointe shoe fitter for a proper assessment.
- **Convertible tights are convenient** when your dancer is moving through back-to-back classes (e.g., from Ballet to Jazz). He or she can just pull the tights off the foot and around the ankle, put on jazz shoes, and hustle into class.
- For convenience, **keep a stock of your child's dancewear, footwear, and accessories in the car.** That way, you can't forget anything at home.

SPECIFIC TO BALLET–SLIPPERS, POINTE SHOES, AND TRAINING

BALLET SLIPPERS

Beginning dancers will use soft ballet shoes, which are slip-ons that typically come with pre-sewn elastic straps. Ballet slippers can be classified into three categories in accordance to the material used, as well as two types of soles:

LEATHER	Full-Sole Ballet Slippers	Split Sole Ballet Slippers
Stiff, stretch, last longer than canvas	Suede covers the entire bottom of the shoe to offer more resistance, therefore, typically worn by younger dancers.	Suede covers the ball of the foot and the heel on the bottom of the shoe (for more advanced dancers), allowing greater flexibility and generally more flattering to the line of the foot.
CANVAS		
More pliable than leather, easier to point foot, don't take long to break in, can be machine-washed		
SATIN		
Wear out much more easily than leather and canvas (aren't customary in present-day dance studios)		

© Can Stock Photo / kornienko

© Can Stock Photo / Coprid

POINTE SHOES

As the name implies, the pointe shoe is a shoe worn by ballet dancers when they dance "en pointe"—that is, on the tips of their toes. Pointe shoes **enable dancers to appear more aerial and sylph-like,** as if they're floating on air.

As dancers advance in ballet, they can graduate to the **pointe shoe which must support the dancer's entire body weight while they dance on their toes.** Each pair should cater to its respective dancer's unique feet, including toe length and shape to the foot's mechanical strength and the arch's degree of flexibility. Quality material and structure is of the essence.

WHAT ARE DEMI- OR PRE-POINTE SHOES?

They are pointe shoes without the shank (the stiff part of the sole). These shoes are intended for pre-pointework and can be thought of as the transition between soft ballet slippers and pointe shoes. There are differing professional opinions regarding the benefits of demi- or pre-pointe shoes; check with your studio to determine their preference.

? WHAT'S SO SPECIAL ABOUT POINTE SHOES?

They are characterized by a hard material ("shank") that runs between the shoe's inner and outer soles and reinforces them in order to support the foot. They are also distinguished by a "box" that encases and supports the toes, and a "platform" upon which the dancer dances en pointe. Ribbons and elastics help keep pointe shoes from slipping off the dancer's heels and add support to the ankle.

To learn more about the many details of the pointe shoe anatomy, search online resources —they're plentiful!

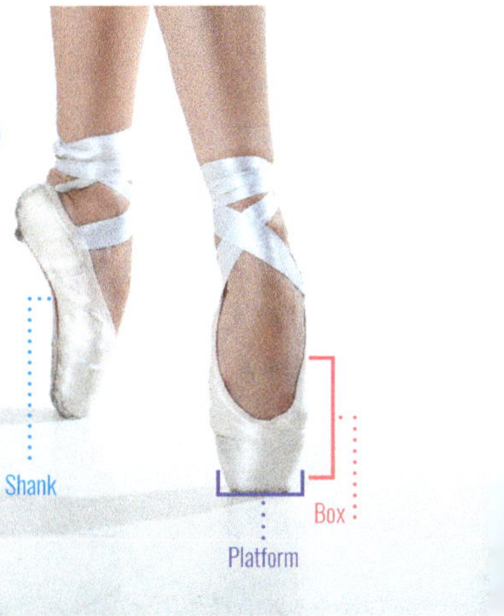

© Can Stock Photo / FotoMaximum

© Can Stock Photo / evgenyatamanenko

PRE-POINTE AND POINTE TRAINING

Pointe training is usually preceded by **pre-pointe training** where the dancer will focus on exercises to develop the technique and strength necessary for pointework. This can be achieved either by specific, pre-pointe classes or by **pre-pointework** during ballet classes. Such training includes building core body strength (primarily of the torso), turnout and alignment, as well as foot, ankle, and leg strength. Demi- or pre-pointe shoes are designed to accompany this training and help the dancer transition from ballet slippers to pointe shoes. However, not all professionals find this type of shoe beneficial.

When a female dancer is told that she is ready for pointe shoes, it is a major milestone and a tremendous source of pride. Many—though not all—female dancers will eventually desire to dance en pointe, making the purchase and use of pointe shoes inevitable. But is pointe training for everyone? There are differing schools of thought among dance professionals regarding whether pointe training is necessary to advance in other dance genres such as jazz, lyrical, or contemporary; some would argue that advanced levels of ballet training—without pointe training—are sufficient.

POINTE SHOE READINESS

Experts will tell you that a combination of age and physical development (weight, feet size and shape, and foot growth plates), skills (training and technique), and strength, stability, and flexibility (core, feet, and ankles) are all factors in determining whether a dancer is ready for pointe shoes.

KEEP IN MIND...

- Although each child is unique, general guidelines for dancing with pointe shoes advise not starting earlier than 11 or 12 years old. Before that age, the bones in the child's foot are still developing and may still be too soft for the rigors of pointework. Of course, just because a child hits the age of 11 or 12 doesn't mean that she is automatically ready for pointework.

Male dancers usually don't wear pointe shoes. There are, however, some roles in the ballet repertoire traditionally performed by a male en pointe.

- Each dance studio will have their own prerequisites for students prior to going en pointe, including—but not limited to—a minimum age, a doctor's approval, x-rays that ensure growth plates are closed, etc.
- Before your child goes en pointe, an instructor evaluation should be conducted. If your child has been studying ballet for a number of years with the same teacher, he or she has already observed your child in class, so a separate evaluation is not necessary—the instructor will let your child know when it's time.
- If your child is not showing signs of puberty but is technically ready for pointework, some ballet instructors will suggest obtaining x-rays of the feet to determine their "bone age."
- Your child may begin practicing en pointe sooner than her peers, which can be a source of contention among dance mates. Discourage your dancer from getting carried away with enthusiasm of her advanced (pointe) training or her ambition—be humble! On the other hand, no need to downplay your child's skills; with the right attitude and approach, a gifted student can become a powerful source of inspiration instead of a symbol to envy.
- If your child begins practicing en pointe later than her peers, remember that—as with life in general— everyone evolves at his or her own pace. Meet with the ballet instructor to learn what is required to reach this milestone and which proactive steps can be taken to help your child progress. Trust the ballet instructor to judge the appropriate time for your child to train in pointe shoes.

THE POINTE SHOE FITTING

Once your daughter's ballet instructor has given the green light, you'll be ready to **make an appointment for your child with a professional fitter** at a local dance shop. Your studio should have a preferred or recommended fitter. If not, survey dance shops in your area to find a suitable, high-quality option.

Photo Credit - Teresa Lee Photography

"I have never seen our daughter more excited about anything in her life than the day she was told she was ready for pointe shoes–she was elated! This moment was a rite of passage."

– B. Houben

WHAT SHOULD A DANCER WEAR TO A FITTING?

- At a minimum, wear tights that will also be worn in class to emulate how the shoes will fit in practice.
- Convertible tights are useful as, when rolled off the feet, the fitter can view the dancer's bare feet and toes.
- Classic attire—a leotard with tights and hair in a bun—allows the fitter to easily see the dancer's lines.

Inquire with your child's ballet teacher or the fitter to learn their preference. Whatever your dancer wears to a pointe shoe fitting—especially your dancer's first one—keep in mind that you'll likely be taking pictures to remember the moment!

The **fitting process** generally involves the following steps:

1. The fitter will **measure your daughter's feet and observe toe shape and length, as well as foot arch.**
2. Based on the initial assessment, **the fitter will select the first pair of shoes** for your daughter to try on.
3. **Your daughter will try the pointe shoes and perform some barre and floor exercises to determine comfort, suitability, and flexibility.** She'll continue to try on different sizes and models until the right one is determined (the pointe shoes should be snug, for instance, but toes shouldn't be overlapping or "crunching" together). The process will be guided by the fitter, who should **pay close attention to your daughter's feedback** while making his or her own assessments.
4. Once the proper shoe is identified, **your daughter will select the elastics and ribbons** that help keep the shoes from slipping off her heels. There are various ribbons, as well as methods of where and how to sew on the ribbons and elastics. Both your dance instructor and pointe shoe fitter can offer tips and help determine what may work best for your dancer.
5. **Your daughter will sew the elastics and ribbons on her pointe shoes**, guided by the fitter.
6. With the pointe shoes fitted and ribbons sewn, **your daughter will leave the shop ready for her pointe class!**

NOTE: SOME STUDIOS HAVE DANCERS SEW ELASTICS AND RIBBONS ON THEIR FIRST PAIR OF POINTE SHOES DURING CLASS AS THEIR TEACHER GUIDES THEM THROUGH THE PROCESS.

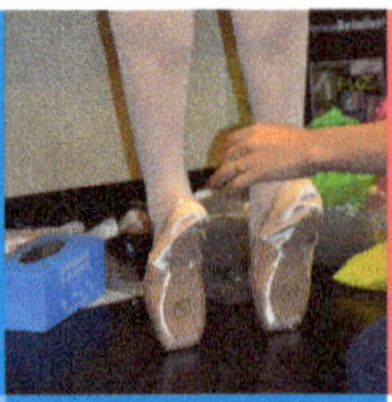

When going to the fitter to choose the right pair of pointe shoes, remember the fitter likely doesn't know your child as a dancer. If the ballet instructor offers to participate in the fitting, it could prove to be a huge bonus!

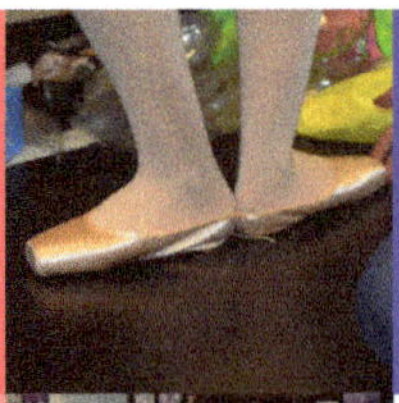

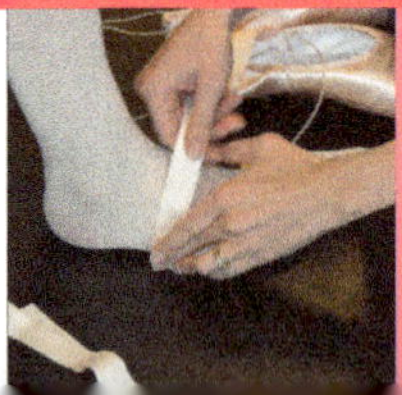

MORE ABOUT POINTE SHOES

The subject of pointe shoes is vast and deep. As a result, there are numerous online resources regarding the topic. For general awareness, let's look at some pointe-shoe basics.

POINTE SHOE BRANDS

Popular pointe shoe brands include Fuzi, Capezio, Bloch, Russian Pointe, Grishko, Leo's, Gaynor Minden, and Freed.

COMMON POINTE SHOE ACCESSORIES

Common pointe shoe accessories (often used to enhance the fit of the shoes to accommodate foot shape and bunions) include toe padding (gel or lamb's wool) or spacers. Ask your child's instructor about recommendations or preferences before the shoe fitting.

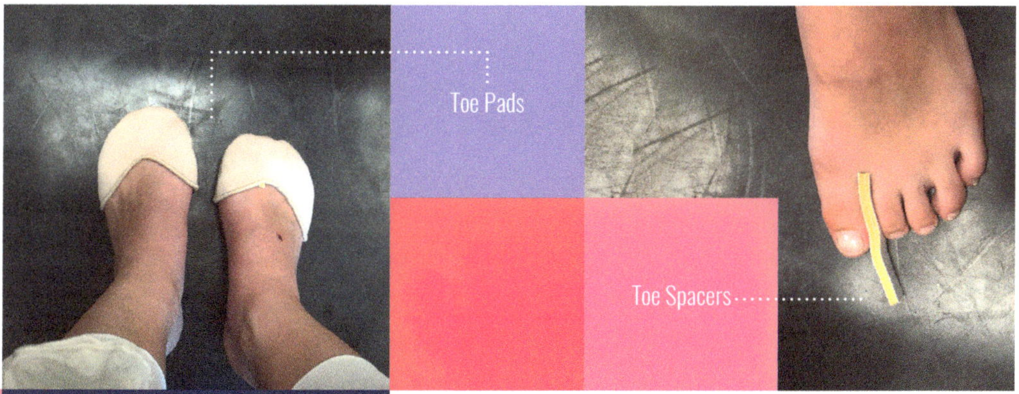

TIP TO AVOID INGROWN AND BRUISED TOENAILS, KEEP NAIL CLIPPERS ON HAND FOR MAINTAINING TRIMMED NAILS.

THE LIFE OF POINTE SHOES

So, your child just got them—now **how long can you expect her pointe shoes to last?**

The **operational lifetime of pointe shoes depends on several variables,** including body shape, foot shape, how intensely the dancer uses the shoes, and which exercise she does in the shoes. Two girls could put on the same pair of pointe shoes on the same day and the overall lifetime of each pair will differ. **You will see your child's individual trend emerge.** It's difficult to predict the longevity of the first pair of pointe shoes, but a pattern will appear after several pairs are worn. Professional ballerinas are known to change their pointe shoes multiple times within a *single concert*.

At some point, pointe shoes will no longer have the structural support to be safe and useful for the dancer. Be aware of when the "box" of the shoe begins to soften and no longer feels supportive or when the dancer can feel the floor through the shoes to an uncomfortable degree while en pointe. These are both strong **warning signs that the pointe shoes should be replaced.**

Dance studios may allow the use of rosin to deal with slippery dance floors, especially when it comes to practicing ballet and pointework—check your studio's policy.

CARING FOR POINTE SHOES

Let your child know that proper maintenance and care techniques can extend the lifetime of pointe shoes:

- Always have clean feet when wearing pointe shoes.
- Keep pointe shoes dry.
- When not in use, place the pointe shoes in a mesh or lace bag to let them breathe.
- Don't wind the ribbons around the shoe which can constrict or mess with the structure of the shoe.

Lace

Mesh

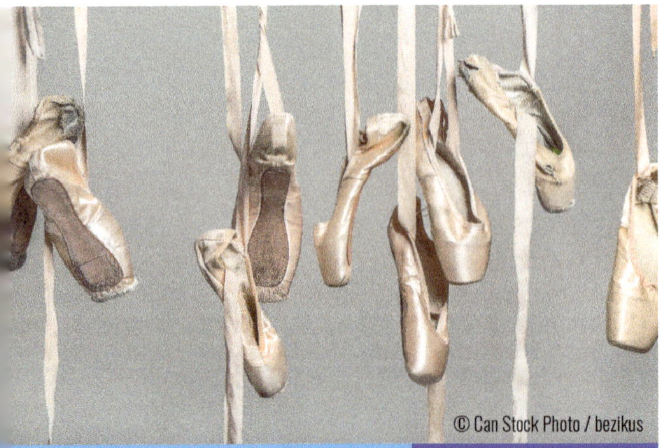

© Can Stock Photo / bezikus

? WHAT TO DO WITH OLD POINTE SHOES?

Many girls like to save used pointe shoes as memorabilia. A first pair of pointe shoes is typically treated in a special way; some dancers place them in a shadow box, a basket, or make them into a pointe shoe mural. Others prefer to de-shank them and use them as soft ballet shoes or embellish them with stones and other decorations, wearing or displaying them as an aesthetic accent (Pinterest has a myriad of respective ideas).

NOTES

WHERE TO BUY DANCEWEAR, ACCESSORIES, AND FOOTWEAR

Shopping for dance clothing, accessories, and footwear is part of a dancer's life. You can find them at

- Your dance studio (if applicable)
- Local dance shops
- Brick and mortar/online stores (e.g., Walmart, Target, Justice, Forever 21)
- Online stores and dancewear companies
- Dance competitions and conventions

There are numerous options. On the following page are some of the popular online dancewear companies you can check out. **Many of these companies also have active social media accounts including Facebook, Twitter, and Instagram–follow them to stay current.**

Photo Credit - Deanna D'Ambra

This is how one mom organizes her daughter's dancewear (which can be a major challenge for a dance family!)

DISCOUNT DANCE SUPPLY

discountdance.com

sugar and bruno

www.sugarandbruno.com

sugarandbruno.com

JUST FOR KIX

justforkix.com

DA DESIGNS Dancewear

dadesigndancewear.com

dancesupplies.com

dancesupplies.com

APOLLA

apollaperformance.com

all about dance

allaboutdance.com

boys dance too.

the dance store for men

boysdancetoo.com

Jo+Jax

joandjax.com

details Dancewear

detailsdancewear.com

DWC DANCEWEAR CORNER

dancewearcorner.com

5

fivedancewear.com

KTRNA KATRINAWEAR

ktrna.com

BDancewear.com 1-888-559-3331

Dancewear Handmade In The USA

bdancewear.com

GetDancewear.com

getdancewear.com

OTHER POPULAR DANCEWEAR BRANDS INCLUDE: DANCEWEAR SOLUTIONS, CAPEZIO, CALIFORNIA KISSES, AND IVIVVA.

BRAND AMBASSADOR

Many dancewear companies offer the opportunity for dancers to represent their company or brand by becoming a Brand Ambassador. These highly selective ambassadorships are usually selected annually via electronic submissions. Once awarded, a dancer is typically featured in the brand's social media campaign and may receive free merchandise with the expectation that the brand be worn and displayed with excellence. Brand ambassadorships may require a non-compete clause or other contract committments. Rules will vary among companies.

LEVEL PROGRESSION

Many dance studios have a **progressive system** for determining and tracking how their dancers learn and grow when it comes to technique. Children are placed within a class adhering to a specific, appropriate level according to their individual capabilities; as they develop, they naturally progress to more advanced levels of dance training.

Examples of how studios commonly structure their **leveling systems** include "Levels 1 – 6," "Levels A – E," or "Beginning, Intermediate, and Advanced." If your child is a beginner dancer enrolled in Tap, for example, the appropriate "intro" class level might be labeled "Tap 1," "Tap A," or "Beginning Tap."

Here is a table with examples of student skill-level and the levels of classes they might enroll in:

	LEVELING SYSTEMS AND SAMPLE CLASSES		
General Skill-Level	**Levels 1-6**	**Levels A-E**	**Beginning, Intermediate, Advanced**
Beginner	Ballet 1	Ballet A	Beginning Ballet
Intermediate	Jazz 3	Jazz C	Intermediate Jazz
Advanced	Tap 5	Tap E	Advanced Tap

LEVEL PLACEMENTS

Level placements are determined by the instructors' evaluations. These are typically conducted at the end of the dance year, although studios may make exceptions and advance a child within the dance year at the discretion of the instructor. Moving to the next level is sometimes a matter of **mastering technique** (i.e., "graded technique" based on a **skills-criteria** syllabus outlining what movements and skills students must learn and master before "graduating" to the next level). Sometimes it's a matter of **age** (e.g., Musical Theater 12+, for children aged 12 and older). **Some studios require students to pass exams to progress to the next level.** To avoid misunderstandings and confusion, discuss the criteria with the instructor so that you and your child understand what's required to advance.

It's important to place your **faith in the dance instructor's assessment** of your child's progression and placement. It's essential to understand that the principle objective is to place dancers where they will benefit most and be most successful. If you have questions about why your child is placed in a certain class level, you have every right to politely ask the instructor for the rationale of his or her decision. **It's important to be informed.**

As in any sport—and as in most aspects of life—**dance has a competitive edge.** Comparing level placements with others is common and can become a source of contention— "Why did she move up and I didn't?" If you find your child in this situation, remember that each student develops at his or her own pace and that your focus should be exclusively on your child's development. As the adage goes, **the only person we should try to "beat" every day is the person that we were yesterday.**

"No one is born a dancer. You have to want it more than anything."
— MIKHAIL BARYSHNIKOV

KEEP IN MIND...

- Progression is most often based on the **mastering of technique, passing exams, age, maturity level, and/or confidence.**
- **A dancer does not necessarily progress to a more advanced level each dance year and may remain at the same level for one, two, or more years** until he or she has gained the necessary skills to progress. Given there are usually no more than five levels at a studio, if a student dances from age five to 18, he or she will inevitably spend more than one year at a certain level.
- **A dancer can become frustrated if he or she progresses to a new level prior to being truly ready.**
- The **leveling process requires trust** in your child's instructor.
- Encourage your child to **focus on a few specific goals** toward advancement.
- Remind a jealous child, **"The only person you should try to 'one-up' is yourself."**

LEVELING SHEET FOR COMPANY DANCERS

ACRO	D/E	JAZZ	C and D
HIP HOP	C/C+	MUS. THE	12+
LYRICAL	C/C+	TAP	C
BALLET	D	POINTE	D- fall

An example of a leveling sheet for an 11-year-old dancer within an A-E leveling system—reflects only the dance genres associated with this specific dancer.

WHAT IS RAD?

The Royal Academy of Dancing (RAD) is an international organization with a curriculum for ballet training accompanied by exams. For more information, go to: www.radusa.org.

WHAT IS ADAPT?

"Founded and owned by Brian and Faye Foley, ADAPT (Associated Dance Arts for Professional Teachers) is a dance syllabus in Jazz, Tap and Ballet created to enhance a dancer's overall technique. ADAPT offers examinations and workshops throughout the year along with a teacher certification course held each July (Teacher's Training School, "TTS"). It's a three-year course that is recognized by the government as a legitimate dance teaching certification program (the only one in Canada). Students can take their exams from the pre-Junior level right up to the Advanced level. In some provinces in Canada, the provincial government and their school boards will recognize high school students' exam marks through the ADAPT syllabus and count it towards their credits for graduating high school—very important for dancers who want to pursue a professional career in dance. ADAPT is owned by Signature Dance Inc."

– Andrea & Ryan Foley

COMMON RULES AND ETIQUETTE

All dance members are expected to follow basic rules of etiquette to keep their "dance family" healthy and happy. Familiarize your child with these good habits. Knowing and abiding by these common **DOS AND DON'TS** can help foster and promote a positive experience within and beyond the dance studio walls.

DOs & DON'TS

- **DO** arrive on time in appropriate attire. This may require arriving at the studio 10-15 minutes early to change or get settled in.
- **DON'T** come to class if you're ill.
- **DON'T** wear street shoes on studio floors.
- **DON'T** wear jewelry (however, medical bracelets and small stud earrings are acceptable). Jewelry can injure your dancer and other dancers and can be lost or broken while dancing.
- **DO** use a black or silver Sharpie® to label footwear, water bottles, and anything brought to dance class with your child's name.
- **DO** bring a labeled water bottle for drink breaks.
- **DON'T** bring food, snacks, or drinks—other than water—into a class. Never chew gum!
- **DON'T** eat during water breaks.
- **DON'T** bring cell phones into class.
- **DO** listen well and keep your focus on the instructor.
- **DO** take and apply corrections from your instructors.
- **DO** be respectful of your teacher and fellow dancers.
- **DO** show awareness of space (don't crowd the teacher or fellow dancers).
- **DON'T** look at the clock often (as if you're waiting for class to end).
- **DO** always ask your teacher before taking pictures or videos during class.
- **DO** ask if rosin (for pointe shoes) is allowed.
- **DO** pick up all belongings after class.
- **DON'T** leave a class early without prior permission from the instructor.
- **DO** enter and leave class discreetly if arriving late or leaving early.
- **DON'T** wear dance footwear outside—the bottoms will get damaged and they can track particles back into the studio and damage the floors.

ANNUAL DANCE COSTS FOR THE EVOLVING DANCER

For planning and budgeting, it's important to be aware of expenses related to dance, especially as your child increases his or her level of commitment. Consider the following scenario within a **single dance year (excluding summer months): one child** taking **six recreational dance classes** (Ballet, Tap, Jazz, Lyrical, Hip Hop, and Acrobatics) and **participating in recital. This is typical for a committed (competitive or performance-based) dancer.**

Please note that **THESE COSTS ARE ROUGH ESTIMATES** and may not include all incidental costs. **Costs across regions and dance studios will vary.** Regarding dancewear and footwear, costs will similarly vary, based on quality and where they are purchased. Keep in mind that each year these costs are likely to increase.

Sample (not actual) **annual costs for a committed dancer for explanatory purposes**

ITEM	DESCRIPTION	EXPENSE
Recreational Dance Costs		
Registration Fee	Due upon registration for recreational classes	$25
Recreational Class	Nine months at $225 per month for six recreational classes	$2,025
Dancewear	One leotard ($25), ballet tights ($15), two dance shorts ($20 each), two tops or sports bras ($15 each)	$110
Footwear	Ballet slippers ($20), tap shoes ($50), jazz shoes ($40)	$110
Annual Recreational Total Cost		**$2,270**
Recital Costs		
Recital Fee	Due upon commitment to participate in recital	$65
Recital Costume	Six costumes, tights, and accessories ($100 each)	$600
Recital Tickets	Five tickets for family members and friends at $15 per ticket	$75
Recital Program	One program book	$10
Recital Pictures	Package C: all class pictures	$50
Recital Gift	Three gifts ($20 each)	$60
Recital Total Cost		**$860**
ANNUAL RECREATIONAL AND RECITAL TOTAL COST		**$3,130**

Your bill will either be emailed to you or available via an automated or online software for invoices and payments.

Your bills will detail costs such as tuition, recital costumes, dancewear, dance shoes, and other dance-related expenses incurred through your studio.

Be sure to check your account statements—a dance studio processes many transactions and errors happen!

"There is something so rewarding about dancing. It's almost spiritual- you let loose, you feel free, you get endorphins from the exercise."
— JULIANNE HOUGH

A DANCER'S HEALTH

As with any athletic endeavor, **plenty of energy and calories are expended through vigorous training and long hours of dance.** It's essential to keep the body rested and healthy. **Make sure your dancer gets adequate amounts of water, food, and sleep**—all three are paramount to reducing the risk of injuries and boosting overall health and wellness. Although every dancer has different nutritional needs, following are some common-sense factors to consider. **For your child's personal wellness and fitness, consider contacting a licensed nutritionist or doctor for a consultation.**

A DANCER'S THREE TYPES OF FUEL

1 FLUIDS

Drinking fluids, such as water or sports drinks that contain electrolytes, is a necessary lifestyle habit that enables a dancer's body to function at its full potential. To convey the importance of this to your child, demonstrate what happens to a plant when you water it and when you neglect to water it. Explain that drinking fluids will help muscles stay supple and help prevent faintness, cramping, and lethargy. Encourage your child to drink water throughout the day.

2 FOOD

The body runs on fuel, just like a car—except, instead of gasoline, our "fuel" is food. Without the proper amount and quality of food, the body simply can't function as effectively, especially when under the high demands of dance. It's important that your child doesn't dance on an empty (or overly full) stomach. Eating small amounts of food throughout the day is a wise technique adopted by many professional dancers to ensure that their bodies are continually fueled with the required energy.

3 SLEEP

Like fluids and food, sleep—or the lack thereof—will always factor into your child's overall health. Follow standard guidelines for your child's age while paying attention to individual needs.

Do not underestimate the physical, emotional, and logistical demands of an evolving recreational or competitive dancer. Check out a typical day in the life of a dancer, which involves keeping his or her body fueled interwoven with school, homework, and dance.

A TYPICAL DAY IN THE LIFE OF A DANCER*

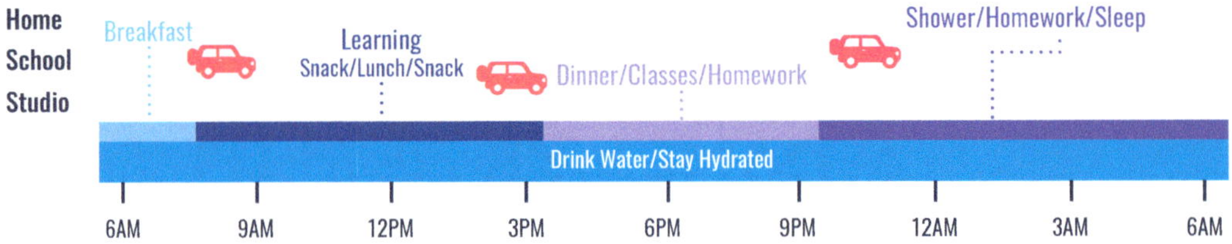

*Pre-professional dancers can be homeschooled, so their schedule will vary, including dance classes during the school day.

THE CONCEPT OF "RECOVERY"

"Recovery from a day of training is essential and requires individual effort. An athlete's body is in a heightened state during times of training and performing high levels of activity. It is important to send the body a signal when it is time to relax. Recovery methods should be utilized at the end of a training day to promote better sleep and muscle repair. Individuals will find a method that works best for them, which may include foam rolling, stretching, restorative yoga, a contrast shower, warm bath, or reading." – Beau Smith, CSCS

> "After training, our daughter enjoys a bath with Epsom salt, an ice bath, or massage – a treat for sore feet!"
>
> – B. Houben

INJURY PREVENTION AND CARE

As athletes, **dancers can work their bodies hard over the years.** Injury prevention should be at the front and center of dance training. Below are common measures that can be taken to prevent dance injury.

STRETCHING and WARM-UP exercises, regardless of the type or genre of dance, should always be incorporated at the very beginning of each dance class so that dancers can loosen their muscles and bodies. Stretching can enhance muscle flexibility, joint range of motion, technique, and body lines. **For each dance genre, the type and amount of stretching may vary.** For example, rolling the ankles and loosening the feet before a tap class are appropriate warm-up exercises.

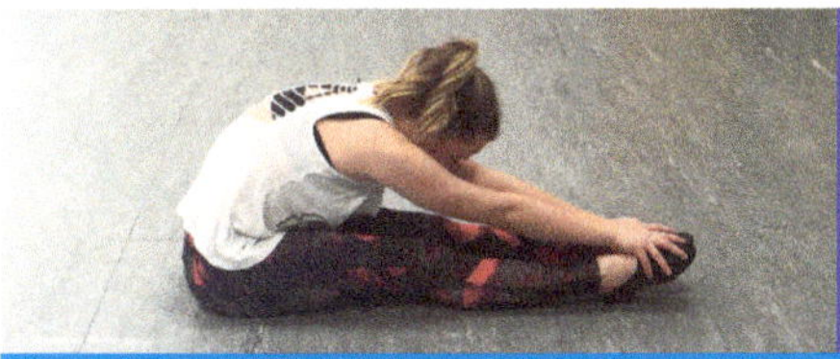

Stretching properly is key to injury prevention!

USING PROPER DANCE TECHNIQUE ensures correct body placement and more control as the dancer moves.

DANCING AT THE PROPER TRAINING LEVEL reduces the risk of dancers pushing themselves beyond their limits.

WEARING QUALITY AND CORRECTLY-FITTED DANCE FOOTWEAR plays an important role in overall fitness and injury prevention. Check with your child's instructor to ensure proper shoe size and shape. Quality street shoes are also recommended for dancers outside the studio.

BEING READY FOR POINTE SHOES is important since wearing them prematurely can be detrimental to the feet. Carefully consider your dancer's age, strength, and development. A teacher evaluation—and possibly X-rays of the child's feet to determine "bone age" —is recommended before your child begins pointe training. (Refer to page 46 for more information regarding point shoe readiness.)

DANCING ON QUALITY FOUNDATION helps absorb the impact of repetitive movements and long hours of dance which can stress joints and bones; a "sprung" or "floating floor" is useful for this purpose. A vinyl composite surface, such as Marley, helps control slipping while dancing.

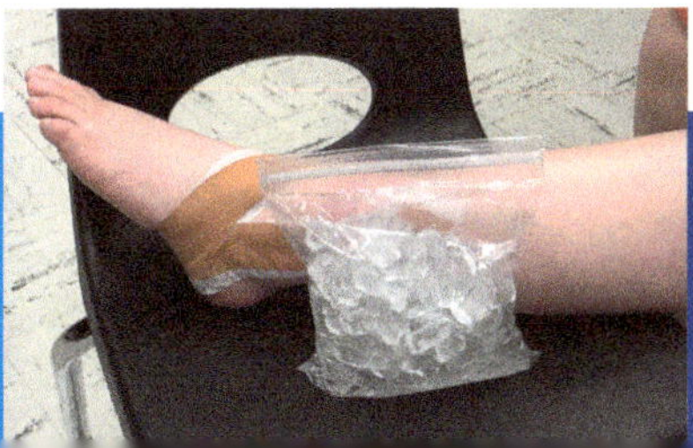

An ankle injury prevented this dancer from going onstage during recital.

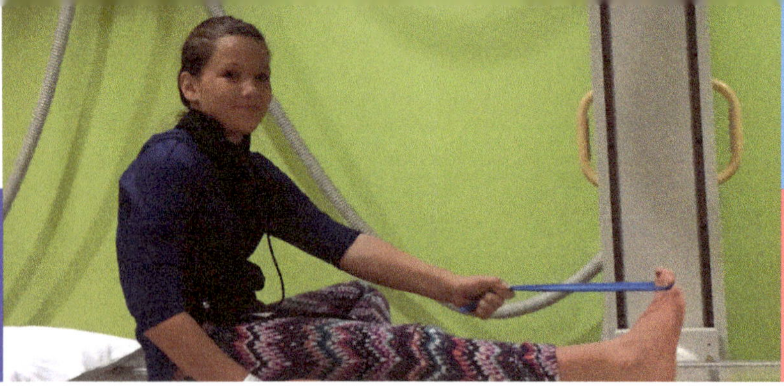

KEEP IN MIND...

- If your child is in pain often and injured repeatedly for no specific reason, it might indicate insufficient or incorrect warming up, stretching, or "recovery."
- Both feet account for 52 of 208 (25%) bones in the human body, which is why taking good care of them—especially as a dancer—is a top priority.
- It's important to know where you'd take your child for care if an injury were to occur.

NOTES

DANCER TOOLS

There are a variety of products to help increase a dancer's **strength and flexibility** while also minimizing the risk of injury. **There is controversy in the industry about how far a body should be stretched and pushed, so it's extremely important for dancers and parents to educate themselves on how to use tools properly and safely—you don't want to end up doing more harm than good!** It is recommended that dancer tools be used under the supervision of a dance instructor, physical therapist, dance therapist, chiropractor, and/or doctor.

No tools are obligatory, and there's no suggestion that you should rush out and buy them immediately. It's just good to know what your options are and to have ideas that you can refer to if or when your child may want them. You and your child can discuss with the instructor which products might be most appropriate. Below are some examples of dancer tools (this is in no way an exhaustive list of what's available in the marketplace):

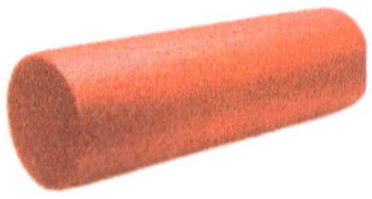

FOAM ROLLER: A brief foam rolling session prior to warm up is a good check-in with the body to see which areas are tight and may need extra attention. For recovery, an extended foam rolling session can help remove tension in the muscles after a long day of training.

TENNIS BALL: A tennis ball or lacrosse ball may be used to help the feet recover from a long day of training, as well as promote joint mobility.

RESISTANCE BANDS: Made of either elastic or latex, these are useful for strengthening and stretching different areas of the body; they're also useful for exercises to recover from certain injuries. These bands come with a variety of resistance levels.

OVERSPLIT TOOLS (overstretch bars, stretch blocks, etc.): Used for achieving oversplits (splits greater than 180 degrees) by elevating the front or back leg while in a split to increase flexibility.

STAGESTEP PORTABLE TAP MAT

Credit: Stagestep | www.stagestep.com

Foam Exercise Roller: © Can Stock Photo / rimglow
Tennis Ball: © Can Stock Photo / Rost9
Latex Resistance Band: © Can Stock Photo / Gismas

ARCH AND FOOT STRETCHERS: Used to improve and strengthen the foot in order to increase the height and shape of the arch.

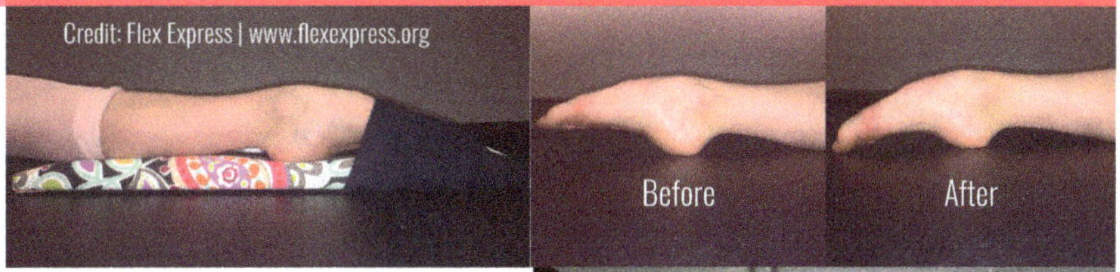

BALLET STRAP:

Used to build strength, increase flexibility, and extend the range of motion.

THE SPIN SPOT™:
Assists in training dancers to spot correctly, find their body's center, proper passé placement, proper core engagement, arm placement, proper muscle memory, and a high relevé.

dot2dance PORTABLE DANCE FLOOR:
A lightweight and portable, genuine dance floor in the shape of a circle covered in typical dance studio flooring, called "Marley". Credit: dot2dance | www.dot2dance.com

KNKMiami by Kimberly Kopke

Credit: KNKMiami | Instagram: @knkmiami
Invented by Kimberly Kopke, Competitive Dancer
Website: KNKMiami.com

SpringCore Balance Premium (Patent Pending)
The SpringCoreBalance Premium is a heavy-duty device that combines the functions of the Pirouette Premium and the SpringCore Balance. By combining the spinning function of the Pirouette Premium and the instability of the SpringCore Balance, you get a device that targets turnout, turning, balance, promenading, ankle strength, hip rotation, back strength, core strength, spotting, proper muscle memory, and control. All in one!

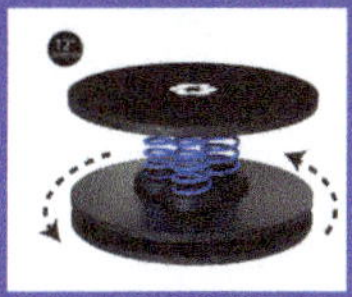

PIROUETTE PREMIUM
The Pirouette Premium is designed to help dancers develop proper body alignment and balance while turning. We consider our larger Pirouette Premium to be the perfect tool for all athletes. It features a concealed, heavy-duty metal spinning mechanism mounted onto a non-skidding lower platform. The upper platform is lined with a non-slip cushion for added comfort while turning. The Pirouette Premium is not just great for ballet practice; our customers have found it helpful for abdominal exercise, break dancing, and more! Don't be afraid to get creative with your Pirouette Premium!

Photo Credit – Photography by Cristy

SECTION 2: THE WORLD OF COMPETITIVE DANCE

Competitive dance is a widely acclaimed and popular sport that involves individual dancers or a group of company members who perform carefully crafted and practiced routines in front of a panel of expert judges for adjudication and appraisal. Competitive dance programs offer an opportunity to **challenge and inspire children** who are serious about dance and who wish to delve beyond recreational dance training and pursue their passion to the next level.

In this section for the Competitive Dancer, you'll learn about

- Selecting a competitive dance studio
- Becoming and being a company member
- Components of a competition routine
- Prepping for competition
- How competitions work
- Dance conventions
- Annual dance costs

> *"By the time I was 4,*
> *I knew how to hit my mark."*
> —SHIRLEY TEMPLE

"Knowing every day, I have an opportunity to do what I love, and find inspiration from all the amazing dancers, teachers and role models I share my journey with, is the biggest gift I could ever dream of. Dance gives you a platform to share your true love with the world, and become a better person along the way."

-MALIAH HOWARD, DANCER, MODEL, AND ACTRESS

FINDING A COMPETITIVE DANCE STUDIO

Your child has evolved through recreational dance and is ready to consider the world of competitive dance. At this point in your journey, you should have a solid understanding of the basics and beyond of recreational dance. If you're part of a dance studio that offers both recreational and competitive programs, you've likely overheard—or spoken to—studio staff, parents, and dancers regarding competition-related dress rehearsals, costumes, competition results, conventions, and more. You've had a sneak-peek into the world that takes dance to a whole new level.

Since there is a lot at stake—time, money, and energy—it's important to think things through and ensure that this is truly what your child desires before making the choice to become a company member.

There are **three basic ways that would allow your child to transition from recreational to competitive dance.** Your circumstances and objectives will determine which option to choose.

1. If you're at a studio that only offers recreational dance, you'll want to search for competitive dance studios in your area.
2. If you're at a studio that offers a competition program, you may choose to remain at this studio (like many dance families do).
3. Even if your current studio offers a competition program, you may consider alternative studios that better meet your child's needs.

"I believe that we learn by practice. Whether it means to learn to dance by practicing dancing or to learn to live by practicing living, the principles are the same. In each, it is the performance of a dedicated precise set of acts, physical or intellectual, from which comes shape of achievement, a sense of one's being, a satisfaction of spirit."
— Martha Graham

THE DANCE YEAR

The competitive dance year never truly ends—it generally starts in August or September and ends in May or June of the following year, plus **summer months** that include competitive dance activities, such as

- Attending a national dance competition for the current dance year
- Participating in intensives and technique training to maintain dance fitness
- Auditioning and learning choreography for the upcoming dance year

As discussed in the Recreational Dance section, most studios are closed for normal business during academic school breaks (e.g., fall, winter, and spring breaks). However, during these periods—to supplement the dance year's regular classes—studios may offer dance training opportunities and private lessons (for individual technique training or solo/duet/trio competition routine practice). Group competition routines may also be rehearsed.

Since it is basically a year-round endeavor, competitive dance involves a considerable increase in time commitment.

HOURS OF OPERATION/CLASS SCHEDULE

Competitive dancers will take recreational dance classes for training, following the hours of operation discussed in the Recreational Dance section. In addition, there are separate company classes during which competition routines are choreographed and rehearsed. Company classes can occur either on a dedicated weekday or during specified weekends. On Sundays, although the studio is closed for normal business, it may hold competitive dance practice for solo/duet/trio or group routines.

PRIVATE LESSONS (A.K.A. "PRIVATES")

In addition to scheduled, required classes, "privates" are classes a dancer takes one-on-one with an instructor or choreographer for

DANCE TRAINING: to benefit from personalized coaching and an opportunity to improve in technique, performance, acrobatics, and other skills (not related to competition routines).

SOLO/DUET/TRIO ROUTINES: to learn, rehearse, and clean a competition routine.

Ask studio staff about the scheduling process and hourly rates (rates may vary among instructors and choreographers).

STUDIO RENTAL

Studio space may be rented for extra practice without an instructor or chorographer (company dancers may want to practice technique or their solo/duet/trio routine on their own). Ask studio staff about the scheduling process and rental cost.

Example of a company with multiple team levels:

Pee-Wee Line
Select Line
Mini Line
Junior Line
Pre-Teen Line
Teen Line
Senior Line

COMPANY LEVELS

Dance studios will offer a competitive program with either one or many levels (teams). A variety of teams allows dancers to be placed in the level commensurate with their skills, age, commitment, and maturity while keeping them challenged. Placements generally occur through an audition process with a panel of studio staff and guest judges but can also be solely based on the assessment of the studio owner/ company director.

An example of a company with multiple team levels:
Pre-Comp (developing skills, less required hours in studio, less company routines, fewer required competition events, regional only competition events)

Elite (advanced skills, more required hours in studio and technique classes, more company routines, more required competition events, both regional and national competition events)

GUEST INSTRUCTORS

Some dance studios offer in-house classes with guest instructors or top-of-the-line professional dancers who visit to teach their students. Such classes can be offered once or several times a year. Benefits include making connections with faculty currently working in the dance industry, gaining new insights from choreographers outside the home studio, and exposing dancers to different dance styles and techniques. Depending on your studio, these classes may or may not be open to non-company dancers.

GUEST CHOREOGRAPHY

Some competitive dance programs bring in outside choreographers to work with company members to choreograph solo/duet/trio and group routines. Typically, the choreographer travels to the studio and teaches the routine, which is then rehearsed and cleaned by a choreographer from the studio throughout the remainder of the dance year. Costs for such choreography will vary and tend to be significantly higher than in-house choreography.

Guest choreographer, Kyle Rostan, with student Sean Lockhart

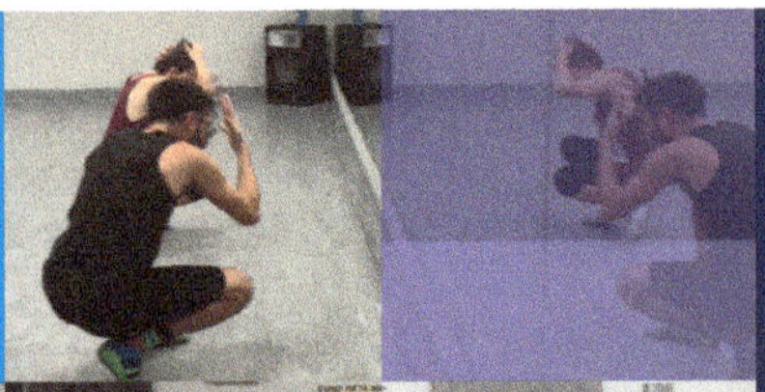

Photo Credits– Martha Lockhart

SELECTING THE IDEAL DANCE STUDIO

Below are overarching factors for parents of **competitive dancers** when choosing a competition dance program for their child:

FAMILIARITY

Assuming your child is enrolled in a recreational dance studio, it makes sense to transition into that same studio's competitive dance program (rendering it unnecessary to seek a program at another local studio). In this situation, your child has already been dancing with company team members in recreational classes, and you've developed relationships with company dance parents; you've become part of the "dance family." On the other hand, if you and your child no longer feel that you are getting the most out of the studio, it may be a great opportunity to consider another studio.

PERFORMANCE EMPHASIS

Most dance studios offer a competitive dance program which includes a wide range of dance genres. Some studios emphasize different characteristics that may be of interest to you and your child:

- A particular dance genre, such as acro, lyrical, or hip hop
- Performance (e.g., a Christmas production, recital, local community events) as opposed to competition
- Higher levels of modesty through costume (e.g., no bare midriffs), choreography, and music selection

TEAM QUALITY AND SUCCESS

Families who become part of competitive dance programs tend to be ambitious in nature and are inclined to be drawn to thriving, winning teams. The quality of the company can be learned by word of mouth or assessed by results of recent competition events found on competition company websites (within the "Results" section).

COST

Cost is a factor for taking on any investment—and competitive dance is no exception. For the competitive dancer, overall financial costs typically include recreational dance tuition, spirit wear, choreography and rehearsal fees, competition and convention expenses (including travel, hotel and meals), and costume and makeup expenses. Prices are generally similar for studios in the same region, but final prices will be studio-specific.

REQUIREMENTS

Each family must assess their ability to meet the demands of being part of a competitive dance team. Common practice for becoming a competitive dance company member involves passing an audition or being invited. Once a dancer is accepted into the dance company, many studios require a company contract to be signed by the dance parent and the dancer. This agreement can include—but is not limited to—requirements such as a minimum number of weekly recreational classes (e.g., eight hours) with a mandatory number of ballet, jazz, or other classes. In addition, a competitive dance team may require commitment to a certain number of competition weekends for regional and national events and summer intensives.

OPPORTUNITIES

Competitive dance programs can offer educational and enrichment opportunities:

- Guest choreographers who travel to a studio to teach classes
- Guest choreographers who travel to a studio to choregraph competition routines
- Conventions where choreographers teach dance students
- Trips to other dance classes in other parts of the country

"Dance is for everybody. I believe that the dance came from the people and that it should always be delivered back to the people." —ALVIN AILEY

STUDIO SELECTION STRATEGY FOR THE COMPETITIVE DANCER

You might remember something similar from the "Studio Selection Strategy" in the Recreational Dance section. Here is an analogous checklist, tailored to your child's developing needs:

1. DO YOUR RESEARCH

- Take the time to survey local studios in your area—including the one your child is already enrolled in, if appropriate—for comparison and assessment purposes.
- Visit studio websites and other social media sites to get a better sense of who they are and what's important to them.
- Read and evaluate online customer reviews.
- Learn about what program(s) they offer:
  - Does the studio offer a performance or competition dance program?
  - Is the competition dance program specialized in a particular dance genre (e.g., acro, lyrical, hip hop)?
  - If a high degree of modesty is important to you, does the program emphasize modest costumes (i.e., no bare midriffs in studio and on stage), choreography, and music?
- Check out studio results from recent competition events that can be found on competition company websites (within the "Results" section).

2. TAKE A TRIP

- Visit each facility which interests you. Although dropping in is typically acceptable, it may not yield the results you desire since studio staff availability may be limited or key personnel may be absent. **Making appointments will ensure that time is dedicated to you.**
- To help with planning and preparing for your dancer's time in studio, does the studio have dressing rooms? A place to study? An eating area?
- Consider the safety of the facility and location. Is there always a qualified adult in the reception area? Are there security cameras?
- Seek cleanliness and overall organization in the facility.
- Seek professionalism in the studio staff.
- Seek input from dance families already attending the studio.

- Are the dance floors "sprung" to reduce the risk of injury by absorbing the impact of repetitive movements and long hours of dance? Is the surface of the floors made of vinyl composite or "Marley" which helps control dancers' slipping?
- Discuss commitments and costs for the upcoming dance year. Request a copy of the company contract.
- Inquire whether the studio participates in any community outreach activities.
- Assess the quality of training, background, and experience of instructors.
- Ask if you can take home a copy of a competition DVD from the previous year to view the quality of the performances.
- Find out when auditions are scheduled to ensure your child is available.

3. COMPARE AND DECIDE

- Compare programs, location, costs, schedule, class size, and the studio's overall culture and environment.
- Compare company requirements/commitments.
- Remember that proper training for the more serious dancer is extremely important in meeting a dancer's potential.
- If your current studio doesn't offer the right program for your child, consider making a change.
- Most competition dance programs require passing an audition or receiving an invitation, so make sure your child has been accepted on a company team before passing up other options.
- Pay attention to your gut feeling and first impression when visiting a studio; it counts much more than you might think. If a studio doesn't feel right for both you and your child, trust your instincts.
- Remember, this is a big decision in your child's future. Many hours will be spent, many relationships will be forged, and a lot of energy and cost will be invested within the dance studio. Competitive dance requires commitment and time; if your child wants to succeed, it needs to become a top priority. Make sure that this is truly what you and your child desire.
- Once a child becomes part of a dance company, it can become a family which makes it difficult to leave for other opportunities that might better meet you and your child's needs. This is a big step—make sure you make a wise choice!

> "Dance has always been a safe place for me. Whenever life was going places I didn't want it to and things seemed to be falling apart, I'd go to the studio and that would be my safe place to let it all go. Dance has given me numerous friends that I can call my family and they have been there for me since the second I walked in those doors. Dance has given me so many blessings and I will always have it in my life, even when I'm 90 years old and can't walk."
>
> – Taylor Blakeley, Dancer

Photo Credit - Photography by Cristy

BECOMING A COMPANY TEAM MEMBER

ARE YOU READY?

The transition into competitive dance shouldn't be taken lightly—either by you or your child. Such programs introduce an advanced level of commitment, time, money, effort, and emotional investment. To decide whether your child is ready to move from recreational to competitive dance, consider the following:

- Does your child enjoy being on stage and performing?
- Is your child showing a genuine interest in competing?
- Has the studio staff encouraged your child to start competing?
- Does your child have the maturity and skillset to participate in competitive dance?
- Can you accept that competition costumes might be out of your comfort zone (e.g., expose the midriff)?
- Can competitive dance commitments coexist with other family activities and commitments, including your child's school schedule and workload?
- How will you get your child to and from the studio multiple times a week?
- Are you prepared to commit to the expenses of time, money, and effort?
- Are you prepared to find bobby pins and hair ties everywhere? :)

© Can Stock Photo / atraks

© Can Stock Photo / brookebecker

"Several years ago, the dance studio that we were at changed their policy regarding choreography. Previously, if a dancer missed choreography, they could make it up at a later date by paying a fee. Then, with a change in policy, my daughter—after being a company member for four years—was told that she could not miss choreography to attend summer camp. She had a choice: go to camp and become a recreational (only) dancer OR don't go to camp, attend choreography, and be a competitive dancer."
– B. Houben

© Can Stock Photo / praisaeng

> "My 13-year old daughter dances 20 hours Monday through Friday, after school, for recreational classes and company rehearsals. There are also additional hours at the studio once a month - "company weekend" - for additional training, intensives, and company rehearsals. And, let's not forget competition and convention weekends about six times per year."
> - B. Houben

AUDITIONS

Auditions for competitive dance programs are conducted to **identify company members and casting** in competition routines. The panel of judges typically consists of the studio owner/company director and teaching staff (choreographers and instructors). Some studios also invite guest judges or alumni to sit on the judges' panel.

Expect to pay a fee for your child to audition for company (e.g., $65). Depending on the dance studio, if your child doesn't pass the audition, this fee may be non-refundable.

During the audition process, you may be asked to commit your child to a maximum number of competition routines, although this number doesn't guarantee your child will be selected for all the routines he or she has signed up for. Some studios predetermine the maximum number of routines for company dancers.

Dancers can be chosen for group routines based on a number of factors:

- Age, flexibility, skills, technical ability, maturity level, attitude, height, body type, and look.
- Splits, leaps, and turns.
- Acrobatic and tumbling skills, including front/back walkovers, front/back handsprings, aerials, and so forth.
- Performance skills (e.g., emotion, facial expressions, and connection to the audience).
- Ability to perform choreography.

CASTING

After auditions, the studio owner/company director will collaborate with the other judges to identify dancers who will become company team members and in which routines they will be cast. This process can take up to a few weeks. Once invitations are handed out, dancers are typically given a period of time to accept or decline any routine in which they've been invited to participate.

Photo Credit - JCM Photography

> "The first company audition for our daughter was nerve-wracking for both her and ME! Luckily the process gets easier over the years." – B. Houben

AUDITIONING – DOS AND DON'TS

When all is said and done, company auditions can be nerve-wracking. Share with your child these common **DOS** and **DON'TS**, which can go a long way towards giving him or her a positive experience.

BEFORE THE AUDITION

- **DO** review the company contract to clearly understand the commitments, should your child become a team member.
- **DO** make sure you can make the audition dates.
- **DON'T** schedule anything high-energy or stressful the day before the audition.
- **DO** be prepared physically; get plenty of sleep and eat a healthy meal the night before and the morning of the audition.
- **DO** come well-hydrated.
- **DO** arrive early, enthusiastic, and warmed up (don't forget to stretch!).
- **DO** know the routines (if given ahead of time).
- **DO** dress in appropriate dancewear so the judges can see the dancer's lines.
- **DO** wear hair off the face and—for older dancers—wear makeup. (When one feels good about how he or she looks, better dancing is likely to follow—it's about confidence.)

DURING THE AUDITION

- **DO** be positive, focused, and serious.
- **DO** smile.
- **DON'T** let anxiety get the best of you—having the courage to try is half the battle.
- **DO** display proper body language and eye contact with those leading the audition.
- **DO** encourage other dancers.
- **DON'T** stand with folded arms or look at the clock.
- **DO** be professional (thank staff after the audition).

DOs & DON'TS

AFTER THE AUDITION

- **DO** relax and be patient as you await the results.

KEEP IN MIND...

- To assess if competitive dance is right for your child, consider signing him or her up for a limited number of competition routines (such as two) vs. the commitment of a high number of routines (such as twelve).
- Being the parent of a competitive dancer requires tremendous involvement, especially during competitions where dance moms are relied upon to support stage-readiness including costumes, hair, and makeup.
- For closed auditions, parents and viewers are not allowed to participate in or view auditions.

"Dancers are instruments, like a piano the choreographer plays."
– GEORGE BALANCHINE

BEING A COMPANY TEAM MEMBER

If your child has auditioned and has been selected to be a company team member, congratulations! Along with growing excitement and commitments, be aware of the additional demands on the body, mind, and wallet. It's advantageous to be prepared for this investment.

CONTRACTS

As aforementioned, to become part of a dance company, dancers and parents are usually required to sign an agreement or contract with the studio. Contracts outline important information that you must agree upon, including time commitments, event commitments, financial commitments, expectations of behavior, a maximum number of allowed class absences, etc.

- Both parents should thoroughly review the contract with your child so that all of you understand expectations and consequences.
- Both parents—especially if separated or divorced—should sign their child's contract, giving them each the rights and responsibilities of the agreement.
- There will be obligations to participate in—and pay for—competitions, conventions, guest choreographers, summer intensives, etc. Make sure you understand your dancer's required availability and the financial commitment.
- Be sure to understand your legal standing upon signing the contract. There could be certain legal fees incurred for breach of contract. For example, if you break the contract, you may be expected to pay a fee which will be applied toward the cost of the choreographer(s) "re-blocking" or "re-staging" the routine(s) without your child. A real-life example was a contract that specified a fee of $100 per routine; the child was in eight group routines, so it cost the family $800 to sever ties with the team.
- If a dancer becomes injured or quits, the studio may charge a fee for re-staging group competition routines.
- It's a privilege and honor to be a company member. A studio may expect or demand exclusiveness and may forbid your child from taking dance classes outside of the home studio or working with outside choreographers.

> Even when injured, company members can still be expected to attend ALL classes and take notes.

You and your child represent the dance studio, especially when wearing the company logo. Always be aware of this, including when posting on social media.

INFORMATIONAL MEETING FOR PARENTS & DANCERS

Company directors typically hold an informational meeting at the beginning of the dance year to provide an overview of the year and outline scheduling events (e.g., competitions and conventions), opportunities (e.g., guest choreographers), expectations, volunteer opportunities, and policies. These meetings serve as excellent forums for parents and dancers to ask questions or gather any information that may have been overlooked.

COMPANY UPDATES

The studio owner/company director typically sends out monthly newsletters—via email, a company website and/or private social media—to keep company members and respective families well-informed of competition and convention events, company fees, costume requirements, rehearsals, volunteer opportunities, and other reminders. A separate calendar, just for your dancer, is warranted to keep track of all commitments.

As the parent of a competitive dancer, it's helpful to be aware of the fact that each studio's company will have its own unique number of team members and commitments throughout the competition season. For explanatory purposes, the below table shows how wide the variety can be.

	APPROXIMATE COMPANY SIZE		
	Small	Medium	Large
# Company members	17	88	140
# Group routines	5	27	80
# Solo/duet/trio routines	0	16	80

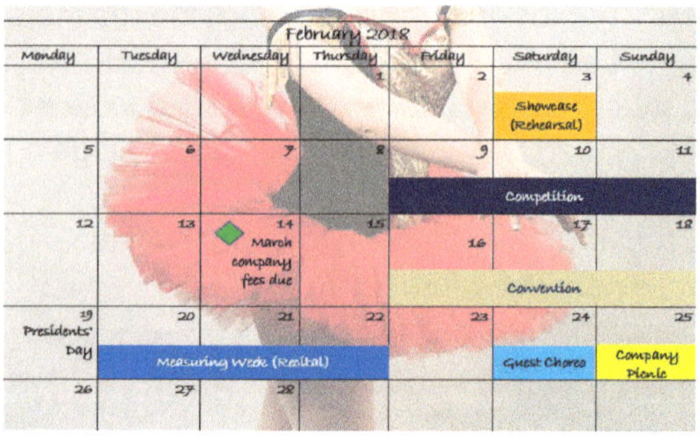

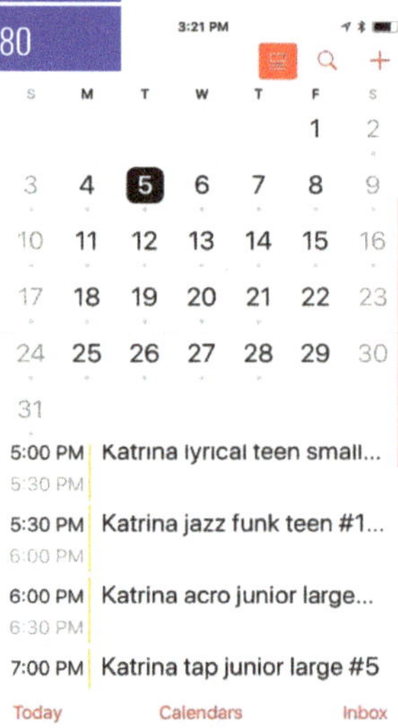

13- year old Katrina's dance calendar captured on her mom's smartphone

Acting for Dancers (AFD) workshop in Parker, Colorado with Sarah and J. Brinson, AFD Founders

"Every year my daughter looks forward to attending the AFD workshop in our region. She leaves invigorated with renewed skills and energy that carry over to her overall dance training."

–B. Houben

YEARLY OVERVIEW

Competitive dance studios attend competitions where dancers perform and compete on stage before a group of judges. Within a dance year, a studio will identify the number of **mandatory competition events** (e.g., four regional events plus a national event) which it will participate in, as well as optional events. Don't be surprised if the first competition happens several months after the start of the dance year—during those first months, dancers will learn and rehearse their routines; staff will prepare costumes, build props, and more. Below is a general timeline for competition seasons—of course, each studio will have a unique schedule.

COMMON COMPETITION DANCE YEAR

DURING THE ACADEMIC SCHOOL YEAR

REGIONALS

Most dance competition companies—often known as "national dance and talent" (song) competitions—put on annual tours with events (also called "stops") in cities throughout the country, drawing dancers from the surrounding area. For example, where we live, there is an annual Bravo! National Dance and Talent Competition event in Denver, Colorado, that draws studios from Denver, Colorado Springs, and other surrounding cities. Regional competitions usually take place over an entire weekend and some studios travel to outside cities to participate in them. **Note: There are some competition companies that do not offer national tours and are based solely in one city.**

Dance **convention companies** also put on annual, regional stops in cities throughout the country. Some conventions are combined with a competition, while others are not. Your company commitment may include one or more mandatory conventions during the year. (See more about conventions starting on page 131.)

DURING SUMMER MONTHS

Once your child becomes a competitive dancer, the level of commitment increases, and summers may never be the same! Time for other activities (e.g., camp and vacations) may become limited, but summer dance activities can be a great way for dancers to continue their training, get to know each other, and bond prior to the competition season.

Summer months for competitive dancers typically include participating in Nationals, intensives, and auditions and choreography for the upcoming dance year.

Dance studios can set their own rules as to which of their routines will participate at Nationals. For some, all dancers may participate. Others may require a specific result in a regional event to quality for Nationals (e.g., placement within the Top 3 Overall with a Platinum score in one of the regional competitions).

NATIONALS

After a tour of regional competitive dance events, "Nationals" is, as its name implies, a nation-wide competition enacted by dance competition companies—such as Starpower, Showstoppers, KAR, and Celebrity Dance—and is generally held over the summer months of June and July. National competitions usually take place over an entire week, and can be up to a 20-hour drive from home. A dance competition company may host Nationals at multiple locations across the country.

Regarding who can participate in a national dance competition, each competition company has its own set of unique criteria, for example—

- An open invitation for all student dancers to participate (no specific criteria)
- Open only to dancers who have participated in their regional dance tour
- Open only to dancers who earn a certain score or placement (e.g., Top 3 Overall) at one of their regional competitions

KEEP IN MIND...

- Not all regional competition tours will end with a Nationals competition. Just so, not all dance studios will participate in Nationals. Inquire with your studio owner/company director or review the company contract to understand if this is a commitment within your annual competition program. If Nationals is part of your child's competition year, you can expect rehearsals to be held (typically) between recital and the competition event.
- Dancers can win certificates at regional events which can cover some of the costs at the competition company's national event.
- Master classes may be offered in a variety of styles during Nationals, often taught by the competition judges.
- Check competition company websites for details.

INTENSIVES

Intensives are rigorous dance training programs designed for motivated dancers and aspiring pre-professional and early-career dancers who seek to improve their technique.

During the summer months, your studio may offer intensives for one or more weeks. Participation is often required for company team members (check your studio's company contract for specifics).

Many professional ballet companies—Joffrey Ballet and the American Ballet Theater to name a couple—offer summer intensives by audition only, with the audition season typically occurring between November and March. Research these opportunities online; they're a great way for students to further their dance education outside their home studio.

SMALLER CLASSES

Summer classes at dance studios tend to be smaller in size, allowing students to get more individualized attention from their instructors. Outside the academic school year, time in studio doesn't compete with schoolwork and other schoolyear activities. Summer can be a time of significant improvement as well as a time to bond with other dancers!

CHOREOGRAPHY

Choreography for the upcoming dance year (sometimes called "choreography week") can start as early as July or August. It's advantageous for all dancers in a routine to be available to learn the choreography. Depending upon the company contract, your child's availability may be mandatory for scheduled choreography; otherwise, your studio may offer a make-up session with or without a fee.

"I dance because it is a safe haven. I dance because I can let go of emotions and let all the bad things go away. I dance because it clears my mind of the bad and fills it with memories of all my friends. It keeps me healthy and strong. It keeps me busy to stay out of trouble. Most importantly it is something I look forward to, because dance means freedom. It fills my day and my life with happiness. It gives me my own touch and my own mark. I dance because it makes me, well me."

- KATRINA LUDWIG, DANCER

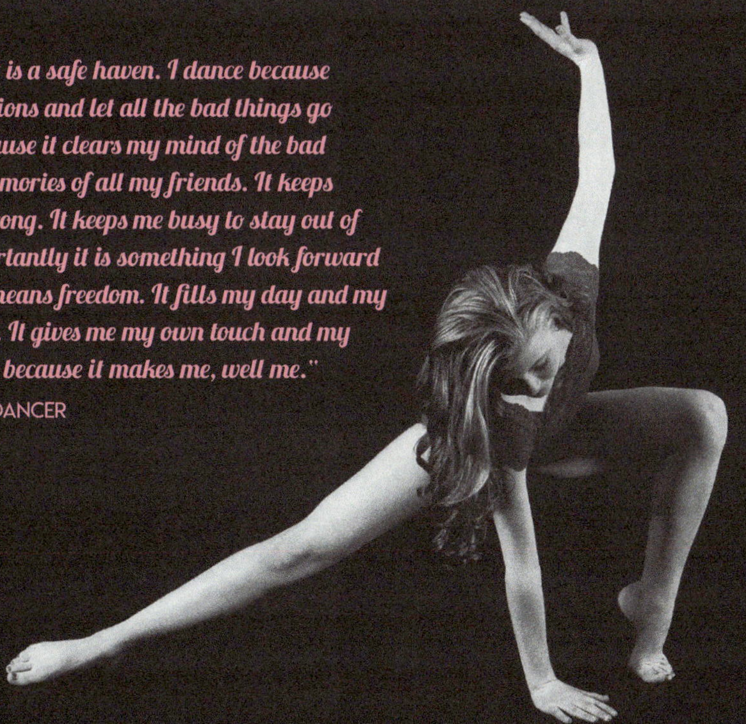

Photo Credit - JCM Photography

Buddy gift!

Dance buddies!

TEAM SPIRIT!

Being on a competition team instills **teamwork** and **camaraderie.** It can bring about a support system and a family atmosphere as the team members spend most of their time together working toward common goals. **Being on a team is an opportunity for a dancer to feel connected and nurture feelings of belonging and purpose.**

DANCE BUDDY SYSTEM

Many studios create a **"dance buddy"** or "mentor" program where an older company dancer is paired with a younger company dancer to provide **mentorship and support.** This program may be called "little sister and big sister" or "littles and bigs." "Buddies" will send notes of encouragement and exchange small gifts during the year, such as at competitions and recital. **This is excellent for team-bonding and forging a healthy, cooperative, and supportive mentality.**

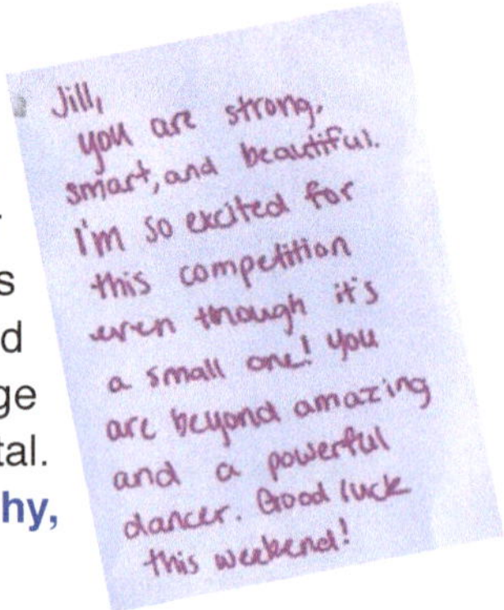

Company pool party!

TEAM-BUILDING EVENTS

Team-building events are valuable for creating and **building bonds and establishing trust** among competition team members. Such events might include a company lock-in (team members spend the night in the studio and watch movies, do arts and crafts, etc.), a barbecue, fundraising activities, and more.

COMPANY GEAR

Company gear with the studio name and logo (e.g., a jacket, dance bag, and t-shirts) is a source of pride for dancers. Although purchasing some gear items is optional, dancers are typically required to purchase company jackets to identify themselves as members of their dance company. At competitions, **it is customary for dancers to wear zipped team jackets over their costumes while outside the dressing room and during awards ceremonies.** In addition to a company jacket, some studios require team members to carry company backpacks or bags. Expenses for company gear are studio-specific and can range from $50 to $200—typically, these products last more than one dance season.

COMPANY PICTURES

Priceless memories of company routines and team moments can be captured within photographs. Studios typically hire a local, professional photographer to take pictures of each company group routine. All company dancers are requested to be present so the studio and team members have a picture of the entire group. Purchasing company pictures may or may not be optional. Check with your studio for specifics.

NOTES

"I do not try to dance better than anyone else. I only try to dance better than myself."
— MIKHAIL BARYSHNIKOV

FEATURES OF A COMPETITION ROUTINE

Competition routines are made up of several elements including entry division, performance division, entry level, age division, choreography, music, costumes, and props. This section is meant to provide a detailed explanation of each element. Although **each studio will follow its own unique method,** below is a table outlining a list of elements of both group and solo/duet/trio routines, as well as identifying who is **typically** responsible for classifying these routines into categories.

ELEMENT	GROUP ROUTINES	SOLO/DUET/TRIO ROUTINES
Entry Division/ Category	Studio owner, company director, or choreographer	Studio owner, company director, or choreographer
Performance Division/ Category	Studio owner, company director, or choreographer	Studio owner, company director, or choreographer
Entry Level	Studio owner, company director, or choreographer	Studio owner, company director, or choreographer
Age Division	Studio owner, company director, or choreographer	Dancer
Choreography	Choreographer	Choreographer
Music	Choreographer	Dancer, studio owner, company director, or choreographer*
Props	Choreographer	Choreographer
Costume	Choreographer	Dancer, studio owner, company director, or choreographer*

*Depends upon the studio—some will give the dancer the option of choosing this element of a routine; others will require the studio owner, company director, or choreographer to make this selection.

Solo/Duet/Trio Routines are also known as

- Extras
- Privates
- Specials
- Specialties
- Individual Performances (IPs)

ENTRY DIVISION/CATEGORY

Each competitive dance routine will be categorized in an **entry division based on the number of dancers** in the piece.

GROUP ROUTINES:

Each competition company (e.g., Starquest, KAR, BravO!) will have its own set of eligible group routine categories (check competition websites for specifics). For a general understanding, here is an example of group entry divisions:

- Small Group (e.g., 4-9 performers)
- Large Group (e.g., 10-19 performers)
- Line (e.g., 20+ performers)
- Production (e.g., a routine with 15+ performers that lasts at least six minutes in duration and includes multiple dance genres while portraying a theme or storyline)

SOLO/DUET/TRIO ROUTINES:

- Solo (a single dancer)
- Duet a.k.a. "Duo" (two dancers, can be a mix of male and female dancers)
- Trio (three dancers, can be a mix of male and female dancers)

Note: While some studios allow **all** company dancers to perform a solo/duet/trio routine, others limit the number of entries based on

- Age
- Invitation only
- Audition only

Reasons for being selective include a large company size (can't handle more than so many entries at competitions), limited rehearsal space at the studio, or protection of the studio performance quality, competitiveness, and reputation.

Also, some competition companies limit the total number of solo/duet/trio routines that can be entered per studio at a competition event. Your studio may prefer to allow all routines to be entered and, therefore

- Not participate in the competition event.
- Participate in the competition event for group routines only.
- Participate in the competition event and allow a limited number of solo/duet/trio routines based on age, skills, or actual scores from either the previous or current dance season.

Photo Credit – Dance Pixs by Acentric Video

TIP Excluding the "Acrobatics/Gymnastics" category, competitive company rules may include limits on the number of acro tricks that can be contained within another performance category (e.g., no acro tricks can be contained in a Ballet routine, no more than three acro tricks can be contained in a Jazz routine).

PERFORMANCE DIVISION/CATEGORY

Both group and solo/duet/trio routines will be based on a "performance" type. While the following is not meant to be an exhaustive list of performance divisions (given that each competition will have different categories and criteria), here are several of the most common categories:

Acrobatics/Gymnastics	A blend of dance movements and acrobatic/tumbling technique
Ballet	Classical steps and ballet technique
Character	Portrayal of a character—from a play, movie, or TV show—throughout a routine
Cheerleading	Cheerleading style with leaps, jumps, vocal cheering, and precision
Clogging	Clogging technique and style
Contemporary	Interpretive dance including lyrical, jazz, and modern dance elements
Hip Hop	Hip hop ("street" dance) technique and moves
Jazz	Jazz technique
Lyrical	Balance, extension, and control combining ballet, jazz, and modern dance interpreting the lyrics or feeling of the music
Modern	Modern technique and movement to incorporate balance, control, isolations, and extensions
Musical Theater	Dance, characters, or costumes using a "Broadway" or movie musical song (often performed with singing or lip synching)
Open	Routine that doesn't fit into any one performance category but is a combination of two or more performance categories
Pointe	Ballet en pointe
Pom	Precision marching and clean, sharp arm movements with pom-poms
Showcase/Adjudication Only	Routine that is performed for critiques only
Song and Dance	The performer sings while dancing
Tap	Tap technique

ENTRY LEVEL

LEVEL	Competition Experience	#Hours Danced per Week	Skill Level
1	Limited	0-2	Beginner
2	Moderate	3-5	Intermediate
3	Significant	6+	Advanced

Levels were introduced by competition companies to help dancers gain confidence by competing against those with similar experience, commitment, and skills. Conventional (non-convention) competition (e.g. Tribute, BravO!, Starquest) will provide general guidelines; the levels might be based on the number of hours danced per week, the years of competition experience, and/or skill level of the dancer(s). Referencing these guidelines, the studio owner/company director will make the final decision for each group and solo/duet/trio routine, placing dancers where they'll be most successful and have the best opportunity to receive a top placement. For example, if your child is young and a new company member, his or her dance routines may be entered in a beginner category. If your child has been a company member for several years and has advanced skills, his or her dance routines may be entered in an advanced category. Above is an example of competition leveling guidelines:

> Trust in your studio owner/company director's decision on which level they choose to place student dancers; the goal is to place them where they'll have the greatest chance of success.

KEEP IN MIND...

- Each conventional competition company will have its own guidelines, unique naming convention for levels (e.g., for BravO!, the levels are O!verture, Encore!, and BravO!), and criteria. At a competition, it's helpful to understand the entry criteria when it's time for judging and awards.
- Not all conventional competitions with have multiple entry levels.
- Convention competitions (e.g., Jump, Velocity) do not have multiple levels; routines are categorized by age. (Refer to **Dance Conventions** on page 131 to learn more about conventions.)

AGE DIVISION

For a solo routine, the age division will be based on the dancer's age as of a specific date*. For duets, trios, and group routines, the age division will be based on the average age of the dancers as of a specific date. The choreographer may choose dancers for a routine because of their age—to either bring that dance into a lower age category or a higher age category. A typical set of age categories follows:

PETITE	JUNIORS	TEENS	SENIOR	ADULT
(8 & Under)	(9 to 11)	(12 to 14)	(15 to 19)	(20+)

*In most conventional (non-convention) competitions, a dancer's age category is based on his or her age as of January 1st of the current dance year. For example, if your daughter turns 13 on December 31, her age category for the dance year is 13. If she turns 13 on January 2, her age category for the dance year is 12. In most convention competitions, a dancer's age category is typically based on his or her age on the date of the convention.

CHOREOGRAPHY

Choreographers are responsible for developing all key elements that make up a dance routine: casting of dancers, the choreography (the dance steps and movements), music, costumes, and props (if applicable).

GROUP ROUTINES will generally be choreographed at the beginning of the dance year. Once the choreography is "set" (fully defined from start to finish), the dancers will rehearse the routine throughout the year on a dedicated day of the week (what's known as a "company" or "team" night) or during specified weekends.

Expenses for group choreography include a fixed fee (e.g., $25/routine) at the beginning of the year and a recurring rehearsal fee (e.g., $25 per routine or per month) throughout the dance year. Rates will vary by studio and choreographer.

SOLO/DUET/TRIO ROUTINES are also usually choreographed at the beginning of the dance year. Once the choreography is set, the dancers will rehearse the routine with the choreographer throughout the year during scheduled sessions. Per the company contract, there may be a minimum number of hours required per month (e.g., one hour per month) for rehearsals.

Expenses for choreography will include a fixed fee (e.g., $150/routine, divided by the number of dancers for solo, duet, or trio) at the beginning of the year and a recurring rehearsal fee (e.g., $70/hour divided by the number of dancers for solo, duet, or trio). Rates will vary by studio and choreographer.

» TIP: WHEN INVITED TO VIDEOTAPE YOUR CHILD'S ROUTINE DURING REHEARSALS, STAND AT THE BACK OF THE STUDIO ROOM AND FILM INTO THE MIRROR. «

CHOREOGRAPHY TERMS:

As the dancers work through a routine, they will inevitably "mark" the routine, perform the routine "full-out," and "clean" the routine.

Marking is to perform a dance routine at full speed to the music while using smaller, less energetic movements. Marking saves energy while allowing the dancers to focus on the timing and placement of the movements with the music. Common practice includes never marking arms (i.e., marking involves going full-out with arms.)

Full-Out is to perform a routine with full energy and effort.

Cleaning refers to polishing a routine and making it "cleaner" in terms of the quality of dance movements and for the clarification of physical spacing and timing. Cleaning can include ensuring that all dancers are performing on the same counts, fine-tuning the arm positions, correcting tricks such as leaps and turns, etc. The routine is broken down into smaller sections and worked until it's "clean."

MUSIC

Music goes hand-in-hand with the genre and choreography of a dance routine. Here are some general rules of thumb:

- For a group routine, music is selected by the choreographer.
- For a solo/duet/trio routine, at some studios, the dancer(s) will be given the opportunity to choose the music; at others, the choreographer will make the music selection.
- Each competition event will specify a minimum and maximum duration of the routine (song). Time limits on routines will likely vary by entry division (e.g., solo vs. small group vs. large group, etc.).
- Most music is "cut" or modified to remove unwanted length, sections, or lyrics. There is music editing software that choreographers can use for this purpose. Cuts in music should be smooth and inconspicuous.
- Your dance studio must obtain proper licensing of songs used in performances.
- In every case, the selection of music must be age-appropriate. The studio owner/company director typically approves all music and lyrics to ensure they don't offend the panel of judges.
- The choreographer can provide a copy of the music for your child's routines so he or she can listen to it and practice outside of scheduled rehearsals.
- It's been said that popular music can be challenging for a dancer to live up to (the judges and audience are taken away by the song as opposed to the performance). A well-known song might also be used in several routines during a competition, losing its originality. On the other hand, when judges are not familiar with a song, there is an element of surprise which can add to the excitement of the routine and possibly influence their scoring in a positive way.
- At competitions, expect the studio owner/company director to provide the competition company with music for all studio entries.
- As back-up for solo/duet/trio routines—even if you don't have the prime responsibility of providing the competition company with your dancer's music—bring your own electronic copy, just to be safe!

» TO GIVE COMPANY DANCERS AN OPPORTUNITY TO PRACTICE OUTSIDE SCHEDULED REHEARSALS, CHOREOGRAPHERS OFTEN PROVIDE THEM WITH MUSIC AND/OR A VIDEO OF THEIR ROUTINE(S). «

© Can Stock Photo / Alexmit

Studio prop room

© Can Stock Photo / PixelRobot

> *"I've been dancing since the age of two. I don't really remember it, because I was little, but my mom signed me up and would put me in cute costumes. A lot of little girls get into dancing, but I loved it so much that I kept doing it."* – MADDIE ZIEGLER

PROPS

Props are used to **enhance the theme of a dance performance,** but they are not mandatory. They can include anything from a tube of lipstick, a hat, a bow and arrow, or a swing-set.

If a prop is used correctly, it can raise the point value during a competition performance. If misused, props can lead to point deduction.

Dancing with **props can add to the level of stress for the dancer** because it's something else to master, and it's one more thing with the potential to go wrong. Since props add to the complexity of a routine, dancers will want to rehearse with them in the studio to familiarize themselves with the items before going on stage.

Who pays for props? It depends upon the studio. Typical scenarios for group routines:

- The studio pays for and owns the props (and they can be reused for future dance years)
- Parents pay a fixed fee (e.g., $75) at the beginning of the dance year
- The cost is divided up evenly between the dancers

Props for solo/duet/trio routines are typically funded by the parents, either self-made or purchased.

TRANSPORTING PROPS

Typically, a studio owns a trailer and either a staff member or dance family will use it to transport props for group routines to competitions. If the studio doesn't own a trailer, they may rent or borrow a trailer or truck. For solo/duet/trio routines, dancers are typically responsible for bringing their own props to competition venues. Some studios will offer to transport dancers' props with an associated fee.

Dance dads can step in and ask if they're needed as Prop Dads to help with the handling of props.

An example of how some dance studios handle costume purchases

	Scenario 1	Scenario 2
Upfront Costume Charge on September 15th	$125	
Actual Cost Determined on October 10th	$135	$100
Variance	-$10	+$25
Action	Family pays an additional $10	Studio refunds family $25

COSTUMES

Costumes are required for competition performances and should match the dance genre being performed, while also allowing dancers the opportunity to produce the best movement for the routine. Costumes should be age-appropriate.

COSTUMES FOR GROUP ROUTINES: The choreographer is responsible for selecting costumes for group routines.

COSTUMES FOR SOLO/DUET/TRIO ROUTINES: At some studios, the dancer(s) will be given the opportunity to choose costumes with the choreographer's approval; at others, the choreographer will make the costume selection.

GETTING COSTUMES

To find and purchase dance costumes for **solo/duet/trio routines**, you may have a variety of options depending on your studio's preferences and capabilities:

> Many costumes for boys are purchased locally at their own expense. Boys often wear black or tan dress pants and solid-colored shirts. If in a group routine, the boys' costumes should complement the girls' costumes. Your choreographer will make the final decision on costume selection.

COSTUME COMPANIES VIA THE DANCE STUDIO

- Browse through **costume company catalogs** at the studio or online to search for the costume that meets your needs. Some costume companies require orders to be made by a dance studio with an **established customer account:**
  - **A Wish Come True** (www.awishcometrue.com)
  - **Curtain Call** (www.curtaincallcostumes.com)
  - **Kellé** (www.kellecompany.com)
  - **Revolution Dancewear** (www.revolutiondance.com)
  - **Weissmans** (www.weissmans.com)
- Expect the studio to **mark up the wholesale price** to account for ordering, administration, and handling costs.
- Expect your child to be measured by studio staff before ordering costumes; sizing will need to be confirmed prior to placing an order.

> Although some studios charge families the exact cost of a costume, it is more likely that they'll mark up the wholesale price to account for researching, ordering, administration, and handling costs. Some studios have families pay a certain amount per costume upfront (before the actual costumes are priced-out and ordered). Then, once the actual cost is known, to account for any variances, families will either be asked to make an additional payment or be refunded the difference. Here is an example with two scenarios for a single costume.

INDEPENDENT FINDS AND PURCHASES

- **Order the costume online**

There are many costume companies that don't require a customer (studio) account to order their products:

- **All About Dance** (www.allaboutdance.com)
- **Dancewear Solutions** (www.dancewearsolutions.com)
- **Discount Dance Supply** (www.discountdance.com)
- **Satin Stitches** (www.satinstitches.com)

Dancer working with a local costume designer and seamstress.
Design Credit: Inspired Designs Costumes LLC

Other options for recycled or gently used costumes include

- **Dance Costume Connection** (www.dancecostumeconnection.com)
- **Encore Costume Couture** (www.encorecostumecouture.com)
- **Ebay** (www.ebay.com)

- **Re-purpose (modify) costumes** you already have, or acquire through a costume swap with other dancers.
- **Make the costume yourself.** Check out **Make Your Own Dance Costume** at www.makeyourowndancecostume.com.
- **Hire a seamstress to make a custom costume.** Seamstresses don't need to be local. For example, a dancer in New York can work with a seamstress in California. Custom costume designers include **West Coast Costume Collections, Moffet Originals, First Dance Couture, Inspired Designs Costumes LLC, Patrick J. Design,** and **To Die For Costumes.** If you're ordering custom costumes, turnaround times are typically longer than ordering from a catalog.

Costumes are typically categorized by dance genre. This one was made for a Musical Theater solo.

© Can Stock Photo / casejustin

Credit: THINX | www.shethinx.com

WHAT TO WEAR UNDER COSTUMES & MODESTY

Costumes look best on stage without the indication of undergarments. Aside from being unattractive, they can be detrimental to a dancer's score; judges can deduct points if lingerie or respective lines and seams show during a competition performance. For this reason, some studios don't allow their dancers to wear bras or underwear beneath their costumes (or only allow specific types).

If allowed by the studio and desired by the dancer for functionality and modesty while changing in the dressing rooms or maintaining integrity on stage, here are some tips and hints for incorporating undergarments (needs and solutions will vary based on costume and body type):

- Always **try undergarments on before a competition** to assess the look prior to going on stage.
- **Wear nude-colored, seamless underwear, camisole, or leotard** which can be especially helpful when a girl is wearing a leotard with nc often leaving her feeling exposed and uncomfortable.
- **Wear a bra with clear, adjustable, and interchangeable straps**
- For backless dresses, **wear adhesive bra cups or breast petals.**
- **Safety-pin bra straps** to the costume to ensure that they don't slip.
- **Sew a bra into the costume,** especially if the costume is custom-made.
- **Use duct tape** to minimize "bounce."
- **Use clear, double-sided tape (e.g., toupee tape) or body adhesive** Stays!®) to keep costumes and leotards from slipping or shifting.
- Consider period panties (e.g., THINX) if pads or tampons don't work for your daughter.

Credit: DJO LLC | www.djoglobal.com

TRICKS OF THE TRADE: For costumes that are itchy, consider using an anti-chafing gel, adhesive bandage, felt, moleskin, or athletic or medical tape. Some moms also sew fabric (e.g., satin, fleece, Lycra®, cotton) over the part of the costume that's itching their dancer.

Seamless Camisole

Photo Credit - Danielle Trina Photography

EMBELLISHING COSTUMES

PURPOSE: Enhance the look and add a wow or pop factor! "Embellishing" is also known as "stoning," "blinging," and "bedazzling."

PROCESS: Apply decorative stones to costumes, tights, and other dance accessories (e.g., a hairbow). The decision to stone a costume may be made by the choreographer.

ACTION: Rhinestones come in a variety of styles, sizes, colors, and quality. They are affixed with adhesive (e.g., Gem-Tac™ or E6000®). Discuss your plan with the choreographer. Stoning is usually done by a seamstress, studio staff, or dance moms.

In addition to the cost of purchasing the stones, unless you do the stoning yourself, expect to pay for having someone else affix them onto the costume. Rates vary depending upon the quality of stones and who will be doing the stoning.

OUTCOME: Dazzling enhancements to dance costumes, tights, and accessories will sparkle under stage lights.

TIPS: Many competitions include showmanship and overall appearance as judging criteria; embellishing costumes, tights, and accessories can have a positive impact on results.

Sequins—generally less expensive—can also be used alone or with rhinestones.

Rhinestones can be purchased online, at your local fabric store, or through your dance studio. In general, online purchases will be the least costly alternative.

Rhinestones are generally purchased in packages by "gross," which represents 144 stones of the same size.

If you're not comfortable stoning, ask a fellow dance mom to help, or visit a professional seamstress.

Plan where you're going to place the stones before you begin affixing them, so they are spaced evenly.

Stones plus the process of applying them to a costume, tights, or accessories can add an unplanned cost of up to $75-$125. This may be less expensive than purchasing items that are already intricately stoned.

Rhinestoneshop.com

DREAMTIME CREATIONS

Rhinestone Guy

Sparkle Up with Style

© Can Stock Photo / yupiramos

RESOURCES FOR RHINESTONES, CRYSTALS, APPLIQUES, BEADS, AND TRIM:

GLORY'S HOUSE
(www.gloryshouse.com)

DIYSPARKLE.COM
(www.diysparkle.com)

DREAM TIME CREATIONS
(www.dreamtimecreations.com)

RHINESTONESHOP.COM
(www.rhinestoneshop.com)

RHINESTONE BIZ
(www.rhinestonebiz.com)

RHINESTONE GUY
(www.rhinestoneguy.com)

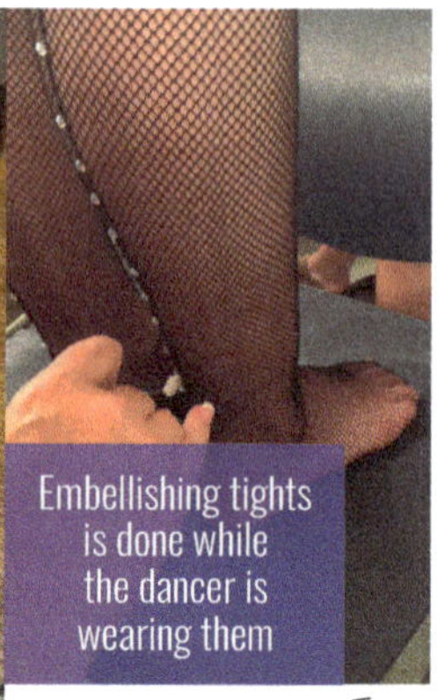

Embellishing tights is done while the dancer is wearing them

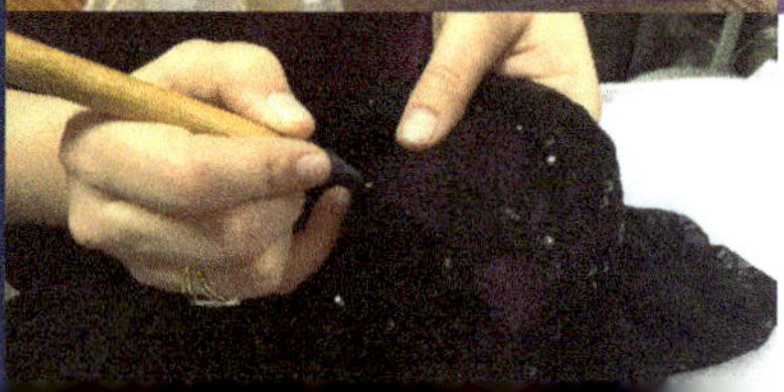

Credit: Eclectic Products
www.eclecticproducts.com

CARING FOR DANCEWEAR & COSTUMES

In support of your child's competitive dancing, a significant investment will be made in dancewear and costumes, so keep them in good condition for current use as well as for giving away or selling when your child no longer needs them.

Dancewear is worn regularly in class and should be washed after every use. Prior to washing, inspect the articles of clothing, and if necessary, **spot-clean first** with a stain remover or with liquid soap. **Follow cleaning instructions on the clothing labels.**

Costumes are a little trickier. They aren't worn as often as dancewear but are generally more complex, so **be careful when cleaning them.** If they get stained, **try to spot-clean first.** Follow the washing instructions on the label, which will vary by type of costume and material. While some parents will dry-clean costumes, others will hand wash or machine wash them inside out in cold water on gentle cycle in a lingerie bag, and hang to dry. **Many veteran dance parents would recommend never machine-washing costumes** as the color may change (and not match the other group costumes); stones, beads, appliques, and especially feathers might fall off or get damaged.

There should be no need to clean new costumes before their first use. It's wise to **be proactive rather than reactive when it comes to costume care,** so the objective should be to not get them stained or dirtied in the first place.

KEEP IN MIND...

- Keep food and drinks away from costumes (especially colored products).
- Have your child wear an oversized shirt or cover-up (button-up, not over-the-head) to protect costumes.
- Apply makeup before your child is dressed in costumes to avoid dripping and dropping makeup products on them.
- Use clear deodorants to avoid staining.
- Avoid perfumes that can stain costumes.
- Let costumes air out after they are used.
- Place the costume in a garment bag as soon as each routine is over.

LONG-TERM STORAGE TIPS

- Before storing costumes, **make sure they are completely dry.**
- Use vacuum-seal bags inside storage containers (this is a space-saving way to store costumes).
- For costumes that must be hung, consider using plastic, padded, or wooden hangers and cover each costume in a dry-cleaning or garment bag. Also, make sure costumes won't stretch out if hung for long periods of time.
- Once stored, it's advantageous to place costumes in a dark and dry area, as sunlight and dampness can affect the material.

TIP:

"Always spot clean costumes to the nearest seam to avoid watermarks."
– Stacy Brisben, Stage Mom

WHAT TO DO WITH COSTUMES AFTER A DANCE SEASON

Over the years, dance costumes tend to pile up! So, what can you do with all of them?

- **Store them as keepsakes,** especially the ones that have special meaning to you or your dancer.
- **Re-purpose them** for a future dance season.
- **Save them and use the materials to sew a quilt** for your child when he or she graduates high school.
- **Give them to young friends or relatives** for playing dress-up or using as Halloween costumes.
- **Give them to fellow dancers.**
- **Sell them to fellow dancers, on eBay, or to costume resellers** to recover some of the expense.
- **Donate them to local theater companies, schools, or hospitals.**
- **Donate them to charity organizations; Traveling Tutus** donates dance wear and costumes to children around the world, and **From Our Hearts to Your Toes** serves children in challenging environments.
- **Sell them to consignment companies** such as Dance Costume Connection.

OPTIONAL ENTRIES – TITLE, PHOTOGENIC, AND OUTSTANDING COSTUME AWARDS

Separate from the traditional scoring, adjudication, and placement of a routine, most competition companies offer additional opportunities for dancers to compete, including for **Title, Photogenic,** and **Costume** awards. When submitting entries for each regional and national competition, your studio owner/company director will ask team members if they want to be entered in these optional contests, which typically come with an associated fee. Your studio will pre-register the interested dancers.

WHAT IS THE TITLE AWARD?

Title is awarded to a male and female soloist—in each age division—who receive the highest score against certain criteria (different from traditional criteria, refer to **Scoring** on page 119) defined by the competition company (e.g., overall performance ability, showmanship, entertainment skills, and overall impression). Title winners become the "Mr." or "Miss" of the competition. For those who participate and value this award, winning Title is a great honor, and—depending upon the competition—the dancer can earn a reward such as a trophy, a tiara (for girls), a jacket or sweatshirt, an award certificate, or free entry into Nationals (if the Title was won during Regionals). Check competition websites for specifics. Some things worth noting about the **Title** award–

- Some company members and studios choose not to participate in this optional entry. Dancers may not want to incur the extra expense, or they may want to avoid the additional competition it breeds among fellow dancers within the same dance studio. For the latter reason, some dance studios frown upon the Title award. Check with your studio owner/company director to see what the studio preference is.
- Depending on the competition company (check competition websites for specifics),

Note: A dancer may not earn a top score (e.g., 1st place) but may still win Title.

various rules apply:

- Soloists can either enter one or multiple (e.g., a limit of three) performances for Title consideration.
- Soloists in the advanced entry division only are eligible, or soloists from other entry levels will also be eligible.
- Only soloists that are registered with a payment are eligible, or all soloists are automatically enrolled at no cost.
- Pre-registration is required prior to the start of the event, or registration at the actual event prior to the scheduled performance can also be accepted.

WHAT IS THE PHOTOGENIC AWARD?

The Photogenic Award is given to the most photogenic contestant and is based on an individual photo submitted by your studio prior to the competition, along with an entry form and fee. Depending upon the competition company, you may be able to submit your dancer's photo at the actual competition event. Typically, the photo requirements include

- A head and shoulder shot
- Size of 8"x10"
- Either color or black and white

Here is an example of a photogenic submission and the associated scoring and comments from one of the judges.

Photogenic submission

Photo Credit – Barefoot Images by Jen

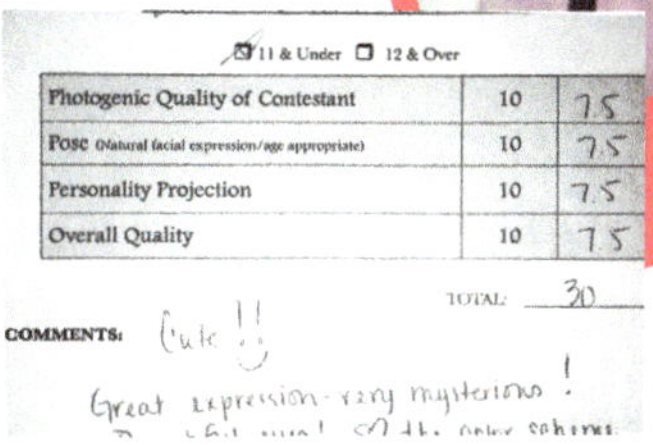

☑ 11 & Under ☐ 12 & Over

Photogenic Quality of Contestant	10	7.5
Pose (Natural facial expression/age appropriate)	10	7.5
Personality Projection	10	7.5
Overall Quality	10	7.5

TOTAL: 30

COMMENTS: Cute!!

Great expression - very mysterious!

Actual photogenic judges' score and comments

Each submission is judged against criteria such as expressiveness of the dancer and the composition and quality of the photo. Winners are typically presented with a plaque and/or an award certificate during an awards ceremony over the competition weekend. Judges' feedback is provided to each contestant.

To be eligible for this award, some competition companies restrict photogenic entries to soloists; others open this award to all performers.

Common practice is for parents to pick up their dancer's photo after the awards ceremony during which the photogenic winner is announced. Check competition website for specifics.

WHAT IS THE OUTSTANDING COSTUME AWARD?

Depending upon the competition company, this award is given to a solo, duet, trio, or group routine where the costume(s) is (are) a stand-out to the panel of judges. It is common for this award to be given out for each age division. Performers may be automatically eligible for this award at no additional cost, or they may be required to register and pay a fee (e.g., $25). If registration is required, your studio owner/company director will ask company members if they want to enter this contest. Check with your studio and check competition websites for specifics.

PREPPING FOR A COMPETITION

Appearance is an important factor in the judging of a competition performance. To produce a uniform, cohesive look on stage, the **studio owner/company director will select the hairstyle, makeup, jewelry, and accessories** to be worn by all female company members for all group routines; for solo/duet/trio routines, there is typically flexibility in choices.

Company members might also be required to wear the same shoe styles. Dance studios may maintain the same "look" year-to-year. If changes are made, it can create a commotion for veteran dance moms who've gotten comfortable with the current requirements—especially the hairstyle!

If you're not comfortable taking on the task of prepping your child's hair, makeup, and accessories, search for online instructional videos or ask other dance moms for help.

HAIR

As mentioned above, each year the studio owner/company director will identify the company hairstyle (e.g., French twist, high bun, high ponytail, center part with low bun, etc.). Young dancers may have a style (e.g., curly pigtails) that is different from the older company members. This company "look" often becomes the studio signature.

Whatever the hairstyle, your dancer's hair should be neat and (other than for something specific, such as a hip hop routine) kept off the face. Judges will notice unkempt hair, including flyaway wisps; which can count against your dancer's score.

Note: Some studios maintain the same hairstyle throughout a competition weekend. Others will require hairstyle changes per a routine based on the genre and costume.

Essential Hair Supplies:
- Hair brush and comb
- Bobby pins
- Hair pins
- Spiraled hair pins
- Snap clips
- Hair bands
- Hair gel
- Hair spray
- Bun "donut," Hairagami™, or fake bun
- Hair net

"I sometimes feel like my daughter has the 'competitive disadvantage' as I am lacking in the ability to apply makeup and do hair that seems so natural to other dance moms. Fortunately, there are fellow dance moms (and older dancers) that are always willing to help us out. Don't underestimate the involvement required and expected of you to support your child in competitive dance including sewing, stoning costumes and accessories, and hair and makeup."
– B. Houben

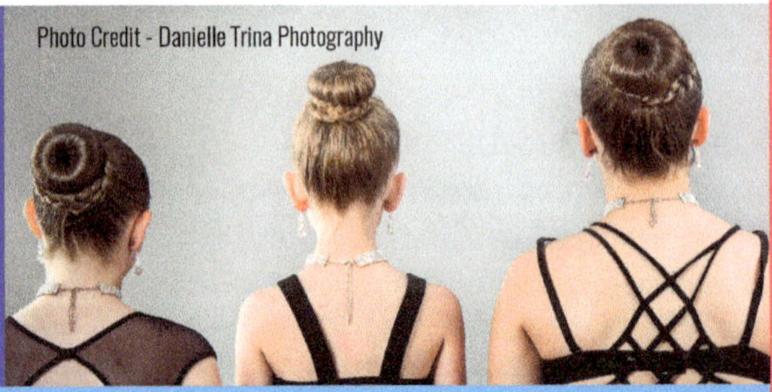
Photo Credit - Danielle Trina Photography

TIP: Pedicures (i.e., filing off calluses on the balls of the feet and heels) before a competition are generally discouraged—they change the way a dancer feels on the stage. For competition, colored nails are also discouraged.

"To dance is to be out of yourself. Larger, more beautiful, more powerful. This is power, it is glory on earth and it is yours for the taking." — AGNES DE MILLE

TIPS & HINTS

- When preparing to go on stage, **ready your dancer's hair prior to applying makeup.** That way you won't have to worry about hair falling in your child's face, and you'll also have a better "canvas" to work with since the light will fall fully on her face and help you see details.
- The hair length of your dancer will play a factor in how easily the style is achieved. Short and unruly hair will take extra effort. **For short hair, consider a fake bun or hair extensions.**
- Hair that hasn't been washed is known to be easier to work with—especially with thick hair.
- Your studio may offer classes to practice the company hairstyle prior to the first competition of the dance season.
- To maintain slick hair, use off-the-shelf hair gel and hairspray products. Or, concoct your own "formula" by taking a spray bottle that's filled half with water and half with regular hair conditioner. Shake it well, and apply it to your dancer's hair. Comb or brush your dancer's hair and apply hair spray. *(If needed for teasing the hair afterward, use **styling powder.**)*
- Check with the studio owner/company director to learn about any **rules regarding tattoos, piercings, hair color, and haircut** which influence the uniformity of a group's look on stage. For example, some studios may require that dancers maintain a "naturally occurring" hair color (i.e., no blue, purple, etc.) during competition season.

CHECK ONLINE TO FIND ARTICLES AND VIDEOS THAT MAY BE HELPFUL IN EXECUTING COMPANY HAIRSTYLES.

PRODUCTS FOR MAKING HAIR BUNS

Ajoy® Bun Maker Donut
Credit: Ajoy LLC

Hairagami™ Bun-Making Tool
Credit: The Hairagami Company
www.hairagami.com

Credit: Whirl-A-Style
www.whirlastyle.com

Photo Credit - Danielle Trina Photography

TRICKS OF THE TRADE: Wondering how to travel with all those bobby pins? Try a hair tie, Ziploc® plastic bag, large Tic Tac® container, pill bottle, traveling soap container, magnetic holder or tray, travel-size Q-Tips® container, or plastic storage containers with compartments.

© Can Stock Photo / schubphoto

MAKEUP

For dancers of all ages, stage makeup is applied heavily on the dancer's facial features to be visible and vibrant under bright and harsh stage lights, especially from a distance—otherwise, the dancer's face can look washed out and tired. The makeup palette (items and colors), brand, and application style will typically be specified by the studio owner/company director. Your child's makeup list may include

- Makeup brush for applying and blending makeup
- Eyelash curler
- Lotion for moisturizing the skin
- Foundation
- Powder
- Eyeshadow
- Black eyeliner
- Black false lashes and adhesive
- Waterproof black mascara
- Blush
- Lipstick and lip-liner
- Makeup setting spray

© Can Stock Photo/ 5second

With the company makeup items in hand, take the following simple steps to get the dancer's face stage-ready for the judges and audience. As mentioned before, your studio may also offer makeup classes or online videos to demonstrate how makeup is applied. You'll find that **there are variations to this process** that are available online and in videos, but sticking to the basic steps below can be just as effective.

ON A CLEAN FACE—

1. **Apply moisturizer to the face and neck.**
2. **Apply foundation to the face that either matches or is one shade darker than the dancer's skin tone; blend lightly into the neck.**
3. **Set foundation with powder.**
4. **Apply blush.**
5. **Apply eyeshadow.**
6. **Apply eyeliner.**
7. **Curl natural eyelashes.**
8. **Apply waterproof mascara.**
9. **Apply false eyelashes.**
10. **Apply lipstick (use lip primer or lip liner).**
11. **Apply setting spray.**

© Can Stock Photo / Laboko

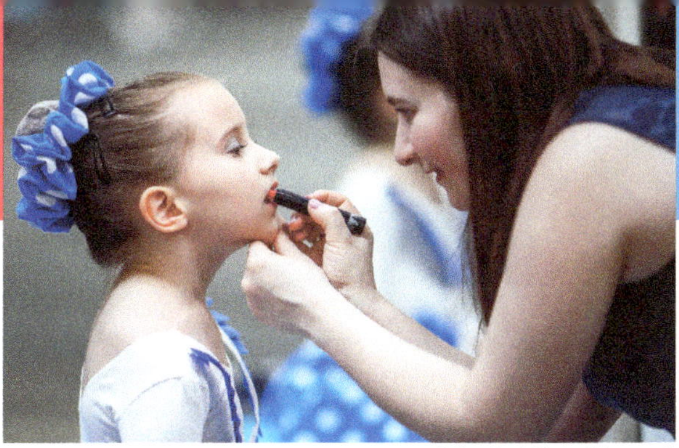

© Can Stock Photo / Veresovich

MAKEUP TIPS

- **Practice** applying makeup before the actual competition event. Some dancers can have allergic reactions, so make sure that makeup is all worked out in advance of the event. **If your child is sensitive to makeup, consider organic or natural products.**
- Apply makeup to a **clean face**—a blank canvas!
- Make sure **eyebrows are defined**.
- **False eyelashes** come in a variety of shapes, sizes and colors; they **can be trimmed** to fit the dancer's eyes (especially those of younger children). They're also reusable.
- In addition to facial makeup, use a **tanning product** or **body glitter** to enhance your dancer's look.
- Eyeshadow, eyeliner, mascara, and false eyelashes are worn to highlight the **all-important eyes.**
- **Clean makeup brushes** after each use rid them of dirt and debris.
- There are numerous **online resources** for how to apply false eyelashes. Below is a process that will do the trick!

» ALTHOUGH NOT A "PRETTY" TOPIC, REMEMBER TO AVOID SHARING MAKEUP TO MINIMIZE THE RISK OF EYE INFECTIONS, COLD SORES, AND SPREADING BACTERIA. «

1. Fit Size	2. Apply Adhesive	3. Let Adhesive Dry	4. Apply False Lashes
Measure and trim the width of the false eyelashes to fit the dancer's eye. If the lashes are too long (width-wise), they can poke, pop off, or drag the eye down. Trim them, if required.	Adhesive (tube or brush-on) is sold with eyelash kits or separately. Apply the adhesive directly on the band of the false eyelash.	Let the adhesive dry for about 30 seconds.	Apply the false eyelash on your dancer's natural upper lash line and press down. Wait a minute or so for the glue to fully dry (the glue will be clear when it dries).

Photo Credit - Danielle Trina Photography

JEWELRY AND ACCESSORIES

Along with hairstyle and makeup, the studio owner/company director will select jewelry (e.g., earrings and a choker) and other accessories (such as a barrette) that are purchased by the dancers and worn at competition events.

TIPS AND HINTS ABOUT COMPETITION JEWELRY

- Putting on earrings can sometimes be sensitive—use Vaseline® or Neosporin® to help ease this process.
- In addition to pierced earrings, purchase clip-ons for when your child's ears become sensitive.
- Adhere moleskin or felt to the inside of necklaces that are uncomfortable around the dancer's neck.
- Buy extra earring backs; they're easy to misplace or lose.
- Keep jewelry in a safe place and keep track of it during competitions —jewelry can be easily lost!

Moleskin adhered to a necklace to provide comfort for a dancer's neck

Example of company jewelry.

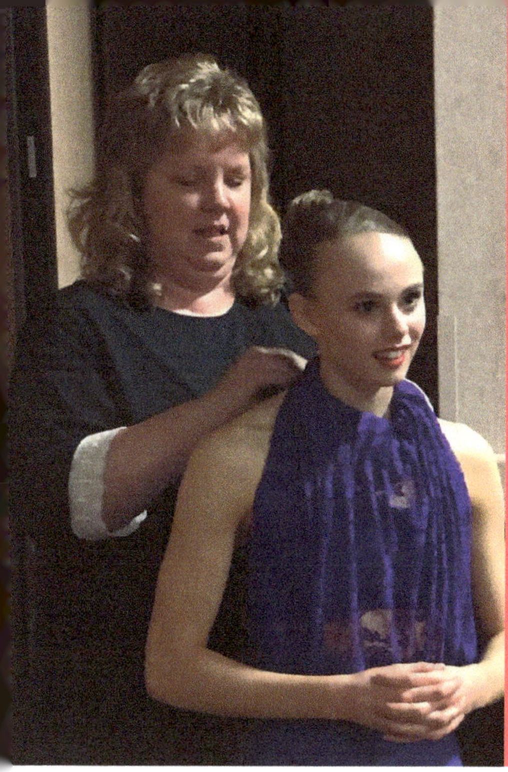

"A few hot tips about preparing for the stage–

Female dancers should ALWAYS make sure they are wearing booty shorts under their costumes. At least once during the annual recital, a student will forget to put them on, so they need to run back to the dressing room. As a stage mom, it's the last thing I ask the dancers before they head backstage.

When handling costumes, don't ever pull a loose thread. This can cause additional damage to the fabric. Instead, cut the thread with scissors.

When a dancer is getting stage-ready, he or she should apply a safety pin wherever the costume fastens together (e.g., velcro, clasps, and fasteners). This provides extra security to ensure the costume stays in place while dancing on stage. Keep in mind that not all safety pins are alike. Check online reviews before making a purchase (if they bend easily, they're not a good safety pin for stage)."

- Stacy Brisben, Stage Mom

NOTES

DANCE PRODUCTS TO HELP YOU STAY ORGANIZED

A competitive dancer has a long list of supplies needed for recital and competition events. **Being organized may very well be the single greatest stress reducer in the face of competition.** To store and transport your things, consider purchasing products that are tailor-made for the well-organized dancer (go online to scout product-specific characteristics and customer reviews to assist in your decision-making process before buying).

DANCE TOWER

Credit: Grit Inc. | www.gritinc.net/dance-tower

Pack2Rack

Credit: Pack2Rack | www.pack2rack.com

Credit: Dream Duffel LLC
www.dreamduffel.com

DIVADOLLY

Credit: Diva Dolly LLC | www.divadolly.com

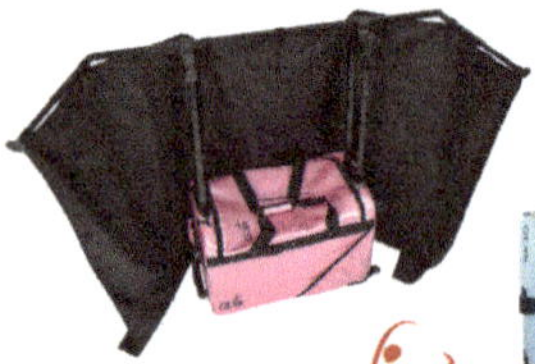

Glam'r GEAR

Credit: Glam'r Gear™ | www.glamrgear.com

The Original rac n Roll

Credit: Racnroll | www.racnroll.com

SIMPLY Caddy

Credit: Simply Caddy | www.simplycaddy.com

RACK MONSTERS

Credit: Level Up Dance Supplies www.levelupdancesupplies.com

TIPS: Some companies will sell factory seconds (products with minor defects) at a discounted price. Some dancers simply organize and transport their dance items by using gallon sized Ziploc® bags with labels for each routine.

The companies listed on the previous page also sell **accessories** and **replacement parts**. Below are some examples of products that **enhance the transportation and organization process.**

Credit: Level Up Dance Supplies
www.levelupdancesupplies.com

Garment bags are used to protect and organize costumes, accessories, and footwear (one for each dance routine). Bags with a clear front are ideal for visibility; zippered pockets are ideal for storing accessories.

Hangers tailored for dance costumes and accessories can make organizing and handling dressing room activities easier.

Credit: Glam'r Gear™ | www.glamrgear.com

Credit: Level Up Dance Supplies | www.levelupdancesupplies.com

Makeup cases are used to store, organize, and transport makeup, supplies, and other accessories. Such organization allows items to be easily found, especially when preparing under time constraints.

Hanging mirrors are very handy for applying and touching up makeup, doing hair, and checking costumes for stage readiness.

Credit: Level Up Dance Supplies | www.levelupdancesupplies.com

Folding Stools are useful when doing hair and makeup, especially at venues that don't have dressing rooms with counters, tables, and chairs.

Credit: Glam'r Gear™ www.glamrgear.com

AIR TRAVEL TO COMPETITIONS

If you fly to a competition location, make sure to **carry on** all costumes, shoes, and accessories in case checked luggage does not arrive with the flight. Fold and pack each costume in a large plastic bag and make sure to separate them from any liquid items.

Credit: Glam'r Gear™ www.glamrgear.com

"Be prepared, work hard, and hope for a little luck. Recognize that the harder you work and the better prepared you are, the more luck you might have." -ED BRADLEY

COSTUME MATRIX

To help you stay organized for competitions (and recitals), create a "costume matrix" which details the costume, accessories, and footwear requirements for each routine.

ROUTINE	COSTUME PIECES	DANCE SHORT	FOOTWEAR	TIGHTS	CHOKER	EARRING	BARETTES	ACCESSORIES
#1 Musical Theater	Top, Skirt	Black	Black Jazz	Black Fishnets	Yes	Yes	No	Double Buns Hair Headpieces
#2 Lyrical	Dress	Black	None	None	Yes	Yes	Yes	None
#3 Jazz Suit	Suit	None	Black Jazz	None	No	No	No	None
#5 Tap	Jeans, Sweater	None	Black Tap	None	No	No	No	None
#6 Hip Hop	Vest, Bra, Top, Skirt	Black	Converse	None	Yes	Yes	Yes	Knee-High Socks

INDEX CARDS

Another idea for being organized is creating an **index card** for each of your child's routines and placing it in the respective costume bag. This will serve as a checklist to make sure you and your dancer remember all the items you need for a complete outfit. You can do this in Microsoft Word by creating a table like the one below, tailoring it to the size and shape desired before printing.[1]

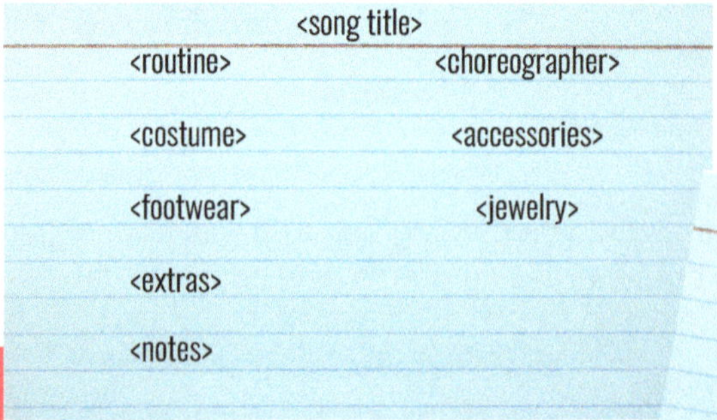

TEMPLATE

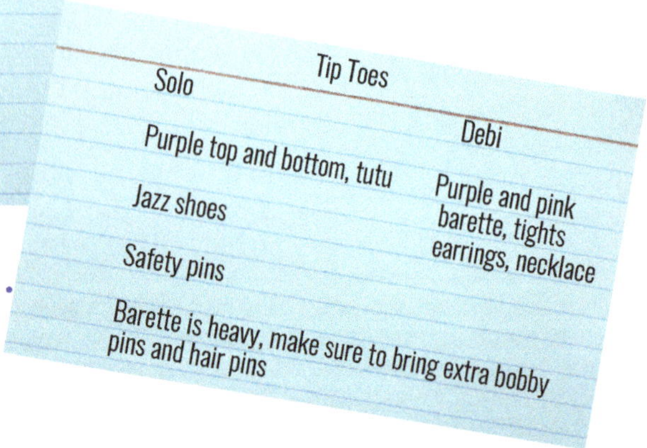

EXAMPLE

[1] Download this template at http://www.bittenbythedancebug.com/

> **TIP:**
> A silver Sharpie® shows up well on black fabric.

SUPPLY PACKING CHECKLIST

COSTUMES/MUSIC/PROPS

- ☐ Costumes
- ☐ Accessories (gloves, etc.)
- ☐ Company jewelry/extra earring backs
- ☐ Company barrette/hair pieces
- ☐ Footwear (e.g., jazz shoes, tap shoes, etc.)
- ☐ Tights (and an extra pair of tights)
- ☐ Undergarments
- ☐ Copy of music
- ☐ Props and poms (if needed)
- ☐ Company spirit wear/company jacket
- ☐ Oversized shirt/cover-up

MAKEUP

- ☐ Hanging mirror
- ☐ Makeup/application tools and brushes
- ☐ Foundation/blush
- ☐ Eye shadow/eyeliner/mascara
- ☐ Eyelashes/eyelash glue
- ☐ Lipstick/primer
- ☐ Glitter
- ☐ Makeup-setting spray
- ☐ Makeup remover/makeup wipes

HAIR

- ☐ Brush/comb
- ☐ Hair pins/bobby pins
- ☐ Ponytail holders/elastic hair bands/hair ties
- ☐ Curling iron/straightening iron
- ☐ Hair spray bottle with water

FOOD AND DRINKS

- ☐ Snacks (e.g., protein bar, nuts, fruit, vegetables)
- ☐ Water
- ☐ Rolling cooler for snacks and water

MEDICINE CABINET/PERSONAL PRODUCTS

- ☐ Athletic tape/bandages
- ☐ Blister & clear adhesive bandages (various shapes & sizes)
- ☐ Lotion/Vaseline® or Neosporin® (for putting in earrings)
- ☐ Ice packs
- ☐ Pain/allergy medicine
- ☐ Contact solution/eye drops
- ☐ Clear deodorant
- ☐ Toothbrush/toothpaste
- ☐ Feminine hygiene products
- ☐ Clothes and undergarments (for leaving competition)

OTHER SUPPLIES

- ☐ Black/silver Sharpie®
- ☐ Safety pins of various sizes
- ☐ Small scissors/needle/thread
- ☐ Clear nail polish and nail polish remover
- ☐ Antibacterial hand wipes/wet wipes/tissues
- ☐ Body tape/body glue adhesive/double-sided tape/moleskin
- ☐ Tanning product
- ☐ Craft/fabric adhesive (E6000® Glue)
- ☐ Extra rhinestones
- ☐ Hot glue gun/glue sticks
- ☐ Stain Remover (e.g., Tide to Go® stick or Parker and Bailey)
- ☐ Pillow and blanket
- ☐ Dancer tools (foam roller, resistance band, etc.)
- ☐ Phone/phone charger/power strip (for sharing outlet)
- ☐ Portable steamer
- ☐ Bluetooth speaker to play music of routines

NOTE: MAKE SURE YOUR DANCER BREAKS IN NEW FOOTWEAR PRIOR TO ARRIVING AT A COMPETITION!

TIPS & HINTS: COMPETITION PREPARATION AND ORGANIZATION

Being organized will significantly reduce stress and promote a more relaxed experience during competition weekends. Below is a list of ideas to get you on your way:

- **Practice** hair and makeup before you head to the competition. It can be a tricky business, so be well-prepared before you arrive to the event (it can get hectic!).
- **Label your child's belongings** (especially dance shoes and even bows and tights) with his or her name or initials using a black or silver Sharpie® (especially helpful for group routines when many dancers will wear the same costume and size).
- **Develop a costume matrix** (see page 104) with a list of routines sorted in order of performance and the associated costume, footwear, and accessories to make sure you don't forget anything. Your studio owner/company director may also provide a costume matrix to team families.
- **Start packing a few days before the event;** if you're missing any items, you'll still have time to replace them.
- **As early as possible, give your child the responsibility of packing, carrying, and tracking costumes and supplies;** have him or her pack using the checklist on the previous page so that they know and remember where everything is. Double-check that he or she has packed all essential supplies. Remember, if necessary, most items can be borrowed or purchased, but not costumes. **DON'T FORGET THE COSTUMES!**
- **To reduce wrinkles, steam costumes** in a bathroom. **Avoid the use of irons** that can burn or melt material.
- **Organize costumes in chronological order** from the first routine of the day to the last.
- Prepare snacks, drinks, and meals for convenience and to keep costs down. **Remember that anything with nuts may affect a child with allergies!**
- **Have easy access to the competition schedule;** print a copy, download a digital version to your phone, or snap a picture of it with your phone. **Know the names of your dancer's routines.**
- **Use a binder** for competition schedules, rules, packing list, hotel and venue information, and costume matrix.
- Bring a list with **contact information** of studio staff, resources, and other attending dance families.
- After a day of competition the dancer and families may go out to dinner, have an after-party, or go to the hotel swimming pool. **Pack a set of clean clothes and a bathing suit** for such occasions.

Here are a few additional tips for staying organized throughout the dance year:

- **Keep a dance binder** with important paperwork including contracts, receipts, calendars, and emails.
- **Keep a calendar** to document all dance commitments and events. Phone calendar apps can be very useful!
- **Keep a log** of expenses and payments.

"If you look at a dancer in silence, his or her body will be the music. If you turn the music on, that body will become an extension of what you're hearing."

— JUDITH JAMISON

SHOWCASE (A.K.A. FULL-DRESS REHEARSAL)

Prior to the first competition of the dance year, it's common practice to rehearse company routines in full costume, hair, and makeup. The purpose of a full-dress rehearsal is to assess the routines, iron out any kinks, and make the dancers feel more comfortable and confident before heading to competition.

Depending upon the studio, the full-dress rehearsal is accomplished either in-studio or as a showcase at a venue with a stage. The studio owner/company director and choreographers will assess—and may even adjudicate—the routines and provide critiques with the intent of applying corrections before the big day! Below is sample feedback for a solo routine performed by an 11-year-old female dancer.

SOME STUDIOS WILL ALLOW FAMILY MEMBERS TO OBSERVE A SHOWCASE, OTHERS WILL MAKE IT A CLOSED REHEARSAL. SUCH REHEARSALS ARE GENERALLY NOT OPEN TO THE PUBLIC.

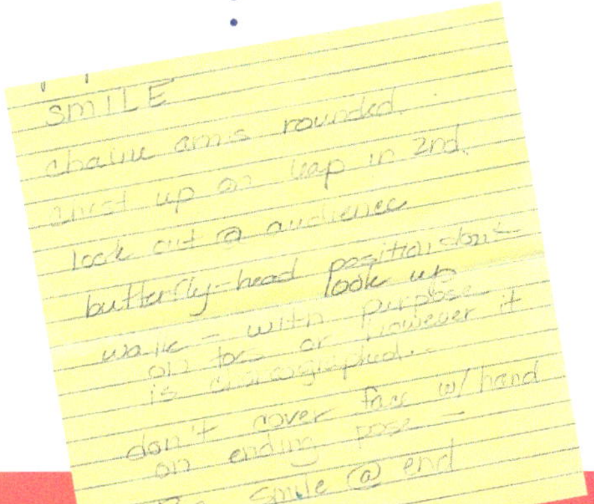

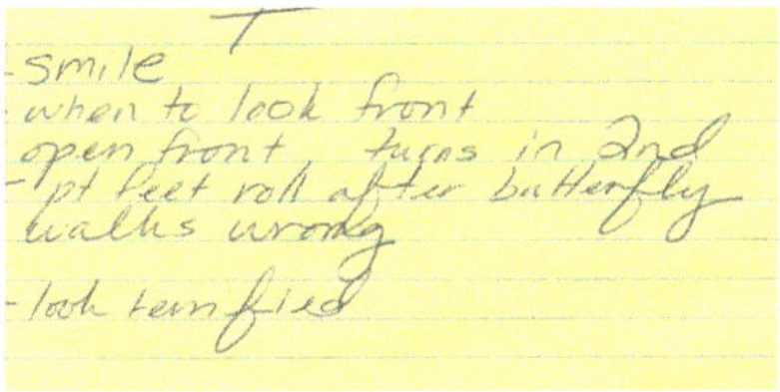

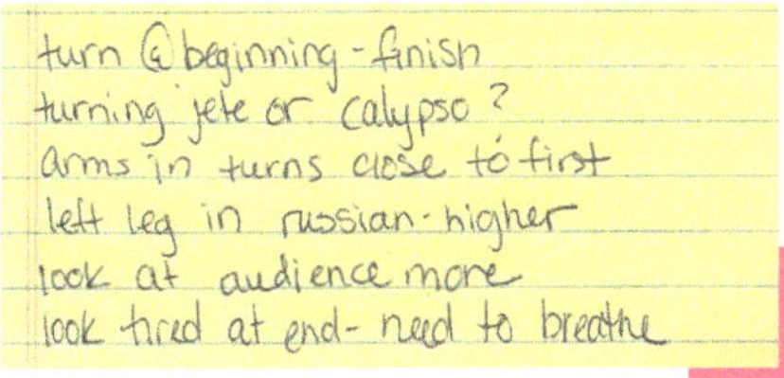

Photo Credit – Rhi Lee Photography

"I could never imagine my life without dance; from everyday classes, rehearsals, conventions and showcases, every chance to dance is a chance to live my best life. My best advice is to remember dance is never about winning, it's always about dancing, so dance and be free and love every second of your journey."

-MAYA HOWARD, DANCER, MODEL AND ACTRESS

BEFORE HEADING TO THE COMPETITION VENUE

Begin preparing your dancer for the competition during the week before the actual event:

- **Confirm your hotel** booking if you are traveling to the competition event.
- **Obtain the hotel and venue addresses and directions** before you leave home.
- Know exactly when you need to be at the event **("call time")** for the first performance.
- Have your child **complete school work assignments** that are due after the weekend so that he or she will be free to focus on the competition.
- Prepare and pack costumes, makeup, accessories, and supplies. **DON'T FORGET THE COSTUMES!**
- **Prepare meals, and pack snacks and drinks.**
- Get adequate **rest.**
- **Leave on time** to ensure you arrive on time!

TIP:

Check to see if there are livestreams of dance competitions. This will allow friends and family to watch your child's dance performances from wherever they are!

Photo Credit – Ashlynn Andrus Smith

NOTES

Note: Each studio has individual rules regarding at what point in the competition season parents are allowed to view company routines, including the following scenarios:

- Weekly, during all practices via viewing windows or CCTV
- Weekly or monthly by means of progress videos
- After a routine is completely choreographed
- At dress rehearsal/showcase
- At competition

Photo Credit - JCM Photography

Photo Credit: Danielle Trina Photography

WELCOME TO THE COMPETITION!

HOW DANCE COMPETITIONS WORK

Dance competition events mix artistry, music, drama, and time-driven activity, along with the element of competition. Your first experience will surely be a whirlwind! Competition days can be long with periods of both busyness and downtime. It may even take participating in several competitions before getting the hang of what's going on—there's a lot to learn and get accustomed to!

Studios—usually ten or so in number—bring dancers from across the city, state, or region who converge at a neutral facility—usually a hotel, high school, or convention center—that can accommodate a large crowd and has enough rooms to provide dressing areas and a stage for dancers. Dancers are expected to be prepared, focused, and ready to compete.

» DANCE COMPETITIONS ARE USUALLY FREE AND OPEN TO THE PUBLIC. «

Although all competition events are generally similar—described in the section below—keep in mind that **each competition company will have their own rules and methods for running events.** Check competition company websites for specifics.

"As a dance parent, you'll likely be running back and forth from the dressing room to the auditorium and so on. I'd suggest wearing comfortable clothing and footwear." B. HOUBEN

"I've been dancing my whole life and it means so much to me. Every time I dance or take the stage I feel full of love and passion. Dance means the world to me and it inspires me to be a better person every day. It helps me become a better person and artist."

— HAILEY MORALES, DANCER AND ACTRESS

COMPETITION SCHEDULE

Before the competition weekend, the competition company will post a **general schedule (or "timetable")** to its website and send it to the participating dance studios for distribution among dance parents and dancers. The schedule can answer some important issues— "Do we need to get there on Friday or Saturday?" or "Can I go home on Saturday, or do I have dances on Sunday?"—and allows for high-level planning. Many competitions occur from Friday afternoon to Sunday evening. Note that each competition event will have its own unique schedule.

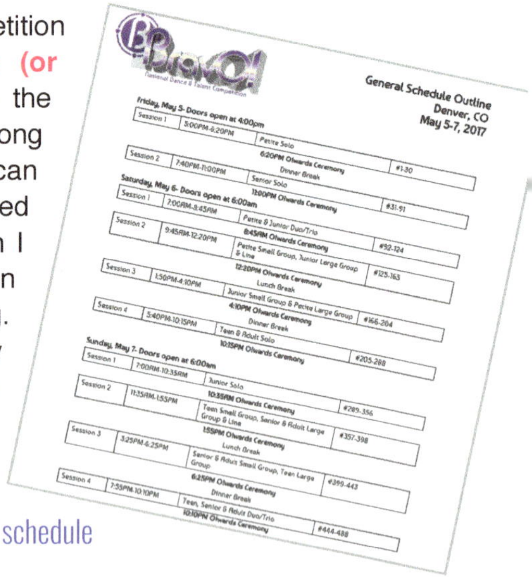
Bravo! National Dance & Talent Competition

General Schedule Outline
Denver, CO
May 5-7, 2017

Friday, May 5- Doors open at 4:00pm

Session 1	5:00PM-6:20PM	Petite Solo **6:20PM Awards Ceremony** Dinner Break	#1-30
Session 2	7:40PM-11:00PM	Senior Solo **11:00PM Awards Ceremony**	#31-91

Saturday, May 6- Doors open at 6:00am

Session 1	7:00AM-8:45AM	Petite & Junior Duo/Trio **8:45AM Awards Ceremony**	#92-124
Session 2	9:45AM-12:20PM	Petite Small Group, Junior Large Group & Line **12:20PM Awards Ceremony** Lunch Break	#125-163
Session 3	1:50PM-4:10PM	Junior Small Group & Petite Large Group **4:10PM Awards Ceremony** Dinner Break	#166-204
Session 4	5:40PM-10:15PM	Teen & Adult Solo **10:15PM Awards Ceremony**	#205-288

Sunday, May 7- Doors open at 6:00am

Session 1	7:00AM-10:35AM	Junior Solo **10:35AM Awards Ceremony**	#289-356
Session 2	11:35AM-1:55PM	Teen Small Group, Senior & Adult Large Group & Line **1:55PM Awards Ceremony** Lunch Break	#357-398
Session 3	3:25PM-6:25PM	Senior & Adult Small Group, Teen Large Group **6:25PM Awards Ceremony** Dinner Break	#399-443
Session 4	7:55PM-10:10PM	Teen, Senior & Adult Duo/Trio **10:10PM Awards Ceremony**	#444-488

Example of a general schedule

A general schedule is usually published a few weeks before the competition weekend. It will typically highlight entry and age divisions (e.g., Petite Solo or Junior Large Group).

" I believe that dance communicates man's deepest, highest and most truly spiritual thoughts and emotions far better than words, spoken or written. "

– Ted Shawn

DETAILED SCHEDULE

At least a week before the competition weekend, expect a more **detailed schedule**—including performance division, entry division, age category, performance order, entry number, routine names, and dancer names—to be published. This will be available either on the competition website or distributed to you by your dance studio. A published schedule is also subject to change.

Segment

Segment Start Time

Entry Division

JUNIOR DUET/TRIO COMPETITION & PETITE LARGE GROUP COMPETITION

10:20AM

JUNIOR DUET/TRIO
JAZZ
AGE 9-11

261. If Mama Were Married
    Jill Capellaci, Mary Terreo
262. Whatever It Takes
    Jesus Hudson, Ally Wilkinson

Performance Division

Age Division

CONTEMPORARY
AGE 9-11

263. Where Do We Go from Here
    Abby Hudson, Heather Smith, Brooke Marie
264. Let me Alone
    Lindsey Allen, Louis Hernandez
265. Love the One You're With
    Sunny Love, Olivia Lynn, Maria Lopez
266. Let me Alone
    Lindsey Allen, Louise Hernandez

PETITE LARGE GROUP
MUSICAL THEATER
AGE 7-8

267. Show Me the Way
    Mary Brass, Sean Cooper, Gianna Cozza, Scott Houben, Michelle Leslie, Julie Martin, Beth Ramirez, Linda Rose, Lisa Schwartz, Donna Thacker, Chloe Wright
268. It Takes Two
    Kylie Bloomfield, Connor Cruz, Amelia Dassa, Seth Jones, Beth Lockhart, Katie Loveland, Enya Perkins, Mimi Scroggs, Valerie Sweat, Rylee Voight, Nick Young

JUNIOR DUET/TRIO
LYRICAL
AGE 9

269. We're Where We Want to Be
    Laurel O'Malley, Sarah Schmidt
270. How Can I Go On
    Stacey Howard, Maya Snow, Suzie Silver

AGE 10

271. On Our Way To The Top
    Molly Sun, Abigail Scott, Mikayla Martin
272. Love Is
    Carly Degani, Wiley Johnson
273. My Heart is Broken
    Bethany Bash, Ella Fernandez, Valerie Top

AGE 11

274. Love it Off
    Krysta Jones, Will Kurtz
275. All the Way
    Grace Walsh, Brenna High

JAZZ
AGE 10

276. Come On, Come On
    Kyla Thomas, Will Kurtz
277. Ice
    Taylor Seat, Emily Blakely

JUNIOR DUET/TRIO AWARDS
PETITE LARGE GROUP AWARDS

Awards

11:50AM

Awards Start Time

Top Score Duet/Trios & Petite Large Group, Outstanding Petite/Junior Duet/Trio Costume

PETITE SMALL GROUP COMPETITION & TEEN LARGE GROUP COMPETITION

12:30PM

PETITE SMALL, GROUP
JAZZ

Note: It can be very nerve-wracking and frustrating to learn of the competition line-up only one or two weeks before the event—especially for dance parents new to competition!

DANCERS MAY NEED TO LEAVE SCHOOL EARLY ON FRIDAY TO ARRIVE PREPARED AND ON TIME FOR THEIR PERFORMANCE.

Photo Credit - King Shots, Inc.

? WHAT IS AN INDEPENDENT DANCER?

In general, an "independent dancer" is a dancer that attends competitions or conventions either without being registered with a studio (i.e., registers under his or her name) or without his or her studio's company team (but still registered through the studio).

There are many varying scenarios that define an "independent" dancer including

- A dancer who trains at one or more home studios in a recreational program but determines his or her own competition/convention schedule.
- A dancer who is a team member of a studio's company but will go "solo" to optional competitions and conventions (being registered by their studio) during available weekends to gain additional training opportunities and visibility (if supported by the studio).

An independent dancer may

- Enter a solo routine at a conventional competition or convention.
- Enter a group routine with other independent dancers at a conventional competition or convention.
- Register for a convention to attend workshops on his or her own.

Since independent dancers won't compete as part of a studio or company, they take the responsibility of performing on their own. An immediate drawback of going solely independent is missing out on being part of a team. The longer-term drawback is that if a dancer wants to dance professionally, he or she should have experience working on teams. Also, not all competition and convention companies take independent entries, limiting a dancer's options.

» CHECK OUT CONVENTION AND COMPETITION WEBSITES OR EMAIL THE COMPANIES DIRECTLY FOR SPECIFICS.

TIMELINE OVERVIEW

UPON ARRIVAL

"Call time" is the time dancers are due at a performance venue for recital or competition events. It's common practice for dancers to arrive with hair and makeup ready within one to two hours of their scheduled performance time. This is because competitions can run earlier than noted on the published schedule (meaning that your dancer may be called to perform earlier than scheduled). Even if the schedule runs on time, arriving early gives dancers enough leisure time to get stage-ready, warm up, and run through their routines with less stress and hassle.

© Can Stock Photo / kgtoh

Upon arrival at the competition venue, expect to come upon a merchandise booth where programs, dancewear, and other items are sold. Many competition companies set up a **media center** with computer screens near the kiosk for viewing and purchasing pictures and/or videos of performances. Check in with your studio owner/company director or a studio representative for any required passes, directions to the dressing room, information about a company warm-up, etc.

Purchase a **program** which contains information about the competition including the names of the host and judges, a list of competing studios, specific order and times of routines, the dancers' names, and scheduled breaks and awards ceremonies.

Programs are handy for tracking the chronological schedule of the competition. They answer questions like, how soon will my child dance? Are we running ahead of schedule? Are we behind schedule? During the awards ceremonies, many parents use the program to jot down the score of each of their studio's and competitors' routines. ***Some families also keep the programs as keepsakes from the event.***

Think twice about inviting your child's friends to a competition—it can be a distraction. Some studios do not allow boyfriends and girlfriends at competition events for that very reason!

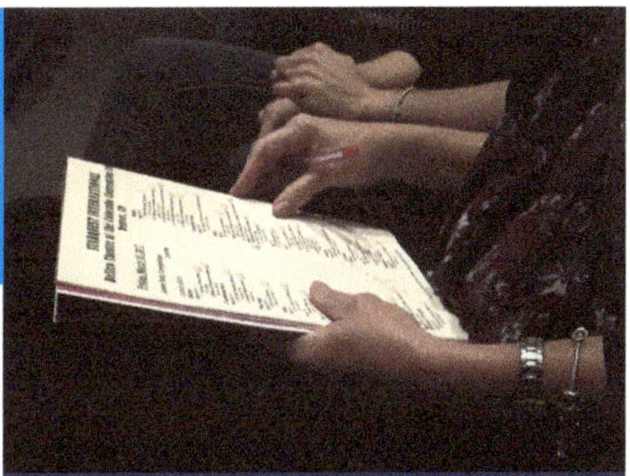

A dance mom tracking the competition program

Directors/ choreographers get settled in the auditorium

The scene of an actual dressing room at competition!

PREP IN THE DRESSING ROOM

At competitions, parents often accompany their dancers to the dressing room, which will most likely be abuzz with activity and preparations. The dressing rooms will be organized in one of the following ways (always separated for male and female dancers):

- Each studio is assigned to a specific room as indicated by signs.
- Multiple studios may be assigned to a specific room (again, as indicated by signs).
- Dressing rooms are open to all studios.

Get settled in and ready to perform! You and your dancer should find a spot in the dressing room to set up your dance rack with costumes in chronological order of the scheduled performances. Lay down a blanket and set out your dancer's makeup case, mirror, and other accessories. If your child hasn't arrived at the venue stage-ready with hair, makeup, jewelry, and dressed in costume, it's time to get him or her prepared for the first routine.

DIFFERENT WAYS TO HANDLE HAIR AND MAKEUP AT COMPETITION

Apply makeup **BEFORE** getting dressed to avoid dripping or dropping makeup products on costumes. With costume changes, dancers need to learn to get costumes on and off without getting makeup on them or ruining their hair.

Apply makeup **AFTER** dressed in costume. Wearing a cape, company jacket, or oversized shirt/cover up can help avoid staining the costume with makeup, hairspray, food, or drinks.

NOTE: TREAT DRESSING ROOMS WITH RESPECT—BE NEAT AND PICK UP AFTER YOURSELF. YOU AND YOUR CHILD ARE NOT ONLY REPRESENTING YOURSELVES, BUT ALSO YOUR STUDIO.

TAKE THE CHOREOGRAPHER'S LEAD. At the appropriate time, the choreographer will come to the dressing room to make sure that dancers are stage-ready. Depending on the studio or situation, choreographers may gather the dancer (for solos) or dancers (for duet, trio, or group routines) to stretch or run through the routine prior to going on stage.

A common sight at a competition is a dancer with his or her parent who is playing the music of the routine as the dancer rehearses his or her routine.

Dancers do a group stretch before going on stage.

Company members taking a selfie!

DANCERS HEAD BACKSTAGE AND PARENTS HEAD TO THE AUDITORIUM

Dancers will head backstage—usually three to five numbers before their number—to wait their turn to perform. They should demonstrate good etiquette by respecting their peers and remaining quiet and non-disruptive while waiting in the wings of the stage.

Parents are generally not allowed into the backstage area with dancers, so now's the time to grab a seat in the auditorium and wait for your child to perform. Check to see if there is a designated seating area for your studio where parents can cheer on dancers together! Make sure you know the names and entry numbers of your child's dances and use the program to keep track of exactly when he or she is going on stage. *(If you don't purchase a program, there's usually one available in the lobby near the media center to reference.)*

DANCERS COMPETE ONSTAGE

It may be easier said than done, due to the anxiety of seeing your child perform or seeing him or her stressed, but (try to) sit back and enjoy! A panel of judges—typically three dance teachers, choreographers, and/or working professionals—will sit before the stage, adjudicate each entry against certain criteria, and submit scores on a scoresheet (written or digital). During each performance, the judges with either write critiques or speak into a microphone and digitally record their critiques (e.g., "make sure you connect on that passé," "oh, nice strong leap," or "I'd like to see more use of the stage"). Written and digitally recorder critiques will be given to your studio after the competition along with the scores, with the purpose of fostering continuous improvement. (Refer to page 124 for more about critiques.)

TIP Make every effort to enter and exit the auditorium in between performances so that you don't obstruct the view of others while they are watching the stage.

Remind your child that good sportsmanship includes saying "good luck" to dancers going on stage, "great job" to those coming off stage, and "congratulations" when they win an award.

AFTER THE ROUTINE IS PERFORMED

Once your child's performance is over, head back to the dressing room to recap the performance, tell him or her how proud you are, and prepare for the next routine, if necessary. Check the competition schedule to learn when the awards segments for his or her routines are scheduled.

» An entry that is "scratched" is when the dancer doesn't perform his/her scheduled routine due to injury, illness, or other reasons.

PICTURES AND VIDEOS

At many competition events, media centers will be setup in the lobby of the venue where digitally recorded photographs and videos of routines can be previewed and purchased. These are great for keeping memories of your dancer's performances!

Digital purchases can either be taken home on a DVD or USB, ordered online, or mailed through the postal system. Options and prices will vary options and prices will vary.

THINGS TO KEEP IN MIND

- Check with the competition company to learn their rules regarding personal photography and videography during the competition is generally prohibited. **If not allowed and someone breaks this rule, this action can ruin a studio's reputation and may even get the team disqualified from the competition.**
- While not typically allowed during the competition, **personal photography and videography is usually permitted during the awards ceremony.** Again, check with the competition company to learn their rules.
- **Personal pictures and videos** of your dancer, their fellow dancers, choreographers, and family members outside the auditorium (in common areas) **are keepsakes!**
- **Competition companies often provide a backdrop** with their name and logo—pictures of dancers are often taken against this background.
- For privacy of the dancers, **avoid taking pictures in dressing areas.**

Check your company contract: Most dance studios will not allow posting pictures or videos of competition costumes or routines on social media until after the first competition OR after the season is over. Your competitors can use this material for competitive research. Also, judges may end up viewing the routine before an actual competition event (i.e., if they are "friends" with or "follow" you, your choreographer, or studio owner), which could put your child in an unfavorable position.

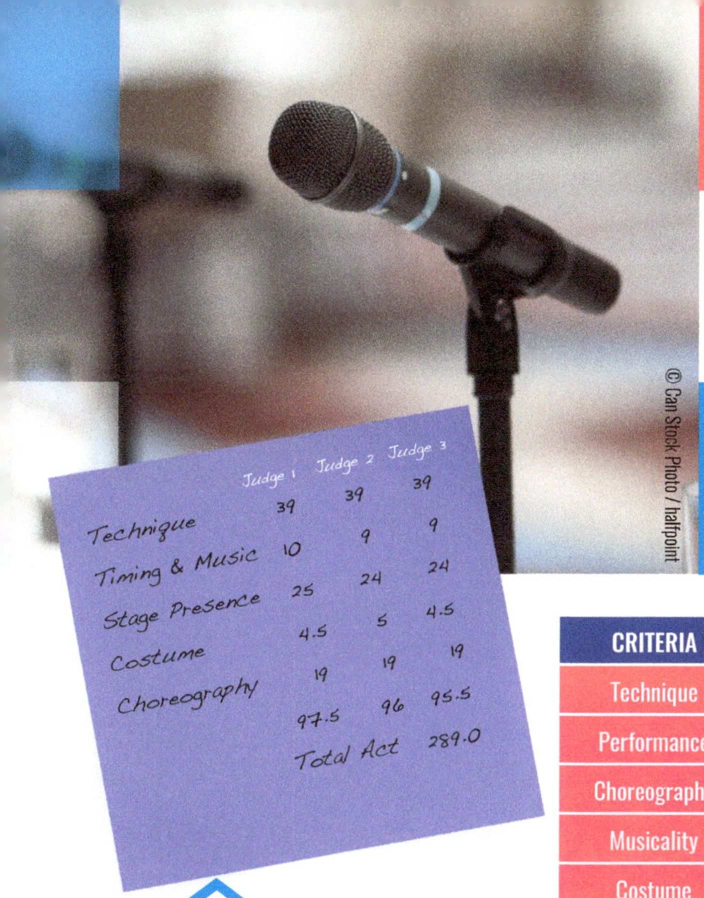

ACTUAL SCORES FROM A COMPETITION

CRITERIA	COMPETITION A	COMPETITION B
Technique	50%	40%
Performance	20%	40%
Choreography	10%	10%
Musicality	10%	N/A
Costume	N/A	10%
Overall Appearance	10%	N/A
TOTAL	100%	100%

SCORING

Each competition will have its own unique scoring criteria and weighting factors that can be found on the company website or in the program. Above are examples of what goes into a routine's final score for two different competitions.

CRITERIA IS DEFINED, MORE OR LESS, AS

TECHNIQUE: correct execution of steps (turns, leaps, extensions, etc.), placement, control, and strength of movement.

PERFORMANCE: emotion, connection to the audience, and facial expressions; synchronization and spacing.

CHOREOGRAPHY: originality and style, connection to the music, formations and transitions, use of the stage, highlights the dancer's strengths.

MUSICALITY: degree to which the dancer hears the music and dances to it (movements become "one" with the music).

COSTUME: suitability to the genre, music, and choreography as well as age-appropriateness.

OVERALL: overall impression of the routine.

NOTE: AT SOME COMPETITIONS, EACH JUDGE GIVES A TOTAL SCORE (E.G., 94/100) AS OPPOSED TO BREAKING SCORES DOWN INTO VARIOUS CRITERIA.

"Dance every performance as if it were your last."
-ERIK BRUHN

© iStock photo / master1305

POSITIVE INFLUENCES ON A DANCER'S SCORE

Dance is different from other sports in that the final score is ultimately based on judges' **opinions and perspectives,** as opposed to scoring points based on meeting certain objectives.

As the parent of a competitive dancer, given that you have a vested interest in his or her performance results, it's helpful to understand some factors that influence a more positive score:

- Clean technique
- Showmanship
- Choreography that captures full use of the stage
- Dance costumes and music that are age- and genre-appropriate
- Connection with the judges and audience
- Synchronization of dancers' movements and the music, as well as correct spacing
- Facial expressions and emotions that match the narrative of the dance
- Well-executed tricks that blend into the narrative of the dance

Judges watch and score dancers from the moment they step on stage until the moment they leave the stage. What is less known to novice dance parents and dancers is that judges are also around the venue before and after the adjudication, giving them an opportunity to observe dancers' behaviors and attitudes (which can influence their impression).

IN ADDITION TO JUDGING AGAINST DEFINED CRITERIA, JUDGING IS SUBJECTIVE—EACH JUDGE HAS A DIFFERENT HISTORY, BACKGROUND, AND TASTE THAT WILL FACTOR INTO OVERALL SCORING OF A ROUTINE.

ADJUDICATION

Each entry in the competition is adjudicated by a panel of judges based on a point scale and will receive a respective award. Each judge has a maximum number of points that he or she can give per the defined set of criteria. And, while **each competition will have its own unique scoring system** that can be found on the company website or in the program, here is an example where each entry can receive a maximum of 100 points per judge:

ACTUAL POINTS					
Criteria	Weight	Max Points Per Judge	Judge 1	Judge 2	Judge 3
Technique	50%	50	48	49	49
Performance	20%	20	19	20	18
Choreography	10%	10	10	10	10
Musicality	10%	10	9	10	10
Overall	10%	10	9	8	9
Total	100%	100	95	97	96
					TOTAL ACTUAL POINTS: 288

Judges' scores will be added together to determine the adjudication. In this example, with three judges, the maximum number of points is 300.

Referencing "Competition A" in the Adjudication System table below, if the dancer receives a total score of 288, the adjudication for the entry will be a "High Gold."

EXAMPLES OF ADJUDICATION SYSTEMS					
Competition A		Competition B		Competition C	
Adjudication	Scores	Adjudication	Scores	Adjudication	Scores
Platinum	291-300	Diamond	93.00+	Platinum	190-200
High Gold	276-290	Platinum	90.00-92.99	High Gold	175-190
Gold	261-275	High Gold	87.00-89.99	Gold	160-175
High Silver	246-260	Gold	84.00-86.99	High Silver	145-160
Silver	231-245	High Silver	80.00-83.99	Silver	130-145
Bronze	216-230			High Bronze	115-130
				Bronze	0-115

THE AWARDS CEREMONY

Throughout a competition weekend, there will be multiple awards ceremonies, each typically held after a "segment" (a group of entries) in the schedule. Segments are typically determined by a target number of entries (e.g., approximately 60 entries per segment). For example, a segment might include the "Junior Solo" and "Small Group" performance categories. All dancers who have performed within a segment will be welcomed back to the stage to participate, wearing their company jackets—zipped and over their costume—to represent their studios. Most studios will require all dancers to participate in their respective awards segment(s). Awards ceremonies are an exciting moment as dancers anticipate and receive their results!

Each awards ceremony typically consists of three main components: **Judges', Adjudication, and Placement Awards.** In addition, awards such as **Title** and **Photogenic** are given out to the winners during one of the many awards ceremonies throughout the weekend (e.g., during the solo awards ceremony for each age division). The Emcee (Master of Ceremonies) of the competition company will announce the awards.

JUDGES' AWARDS

Judges may also give out special awards for routines whose qualities are not related to the criteria of the final score but are based on their reaction to performances—when they see something special about a routine—and want to recognize and reward a dancer or dancers. Some competition companies have a separate "Special Awards" judge for this purpose. Examples include: Best Smile, Most Energetic, Working the Stage, and Showmanship.

WHAT HAPPENS WITH THE AWARDS? (e.g., trophies, plaques, pins, medals, and cash) Although studio policies may vary, here are some likely scenarios:

FOR A SOLO DANCER

- He or she may **take home any awards** received.
- Trophies, plaques, or medals **may go to the studio** and the dancer keeps his or her pin.
- **Cash prizes** are typically credited to the dancer's studio account.

FOR DUET/TRIO DANCERS

- They may take home any awards received. Since only **one award** is typically handed out, dancers have options:
  - They **agree upfront** which dancer will take home the award (and alternate among competitions).
  - They **purchase an extra award** (some competition companies sell trophies, for example, that families can purchase and **split the cost**).
- Trophies, plaques, or medals go back to the studio and the dancers keep their pins.
- Cash prizes are typically **split equally among the number of dancers** and credited to their studio accounts.

FOR GROUP ROUTINES

- **Trophies, plaques, and medals** go back to the studio.
- The captain takes home the pins and disperses them among the dancers at the **next company rehearsal**.
- Some **competition companies sell trophies**, for example, that families can purchase.
- Cash prizes are typically **split equally among the number of dancers** and credited their studio accounts or given to the associated booster club.

Special judges' award

"STYLIZED AWARD"

Judge: "I was so impressed by this routine for its choreography, how beautifully it was executed and how clean and sophisticated it was. This award goes to entry number 327, 'Stutter.'"

ADJUDICATION

Each entry receives an adjudication based on its score. The host of the competition will call out each entry—usually in numerical order—and announce the respective adjudication award (e.g., "Platinum," "High Gold," or "Gold"). For a solo routine, for instance, the host may say, "Entry #39, Tip Toes, Platinum." When called, the dancer will be handed an award (e.g., a plaque or pin) that reflects the adjudication score received.

For group routines, studios may select a **"captain"** (one of the dancers in the routine) to collect the group's award. This role may be rotated among dancers throughout the dance season.

PLACEMENT AWARDS

In addition to an adjudication award for each routine, Placement Awards for 1st, 2nd, 3rd, etc. are given to those routines with the highest scores. Although each competition company will have its own unique award system, many give out Placement Awards for each entry level (e.g., Beginner, Intermediate, and Advanced) and age division (e.g., Mini, Junior, Teen, Senior) by entry division (e.g., Solo, Small Group, Large Group). Here are a few examples:

Advanced (e.g., "Elite"), Teen, Solo Placement Awards: In this case, all Teen, Solo entries in the Advanced level will be ranked to identify the winners of the high placement awards.

Beginner, Junior, Small Group Placement Awards: In this case, all Junior, Small Group entries in the Beginner level will be ranked to identify the winners of the high placement awards.

The winners will be called to the front of the stage (with the first-place winner being called up last) and presented their respective award. Competitions will bring up anywhere from the Top 5 to the Top 20, depending upon the number of entries.

Note: Refer to **Entry Levels** on page 85.

TIE-BREAKERS If the scores of two routines are tied, the tie will be broken by the technique score.

OVERALL SCORE AWARDS

Overall Score Awards are also awarded to the highest scoring (1st Place) entries, typically for each entry level (e.g., Beginner, Intermediate, and Advanced) and age division (e.g., Mini, Junior, Teen, Senior) by entry division (e.g., Solo, Small Group, Large Group). For example, the highest score of all entries in the Beginner (e.g., "Novice") level in the Junior age division for Small Groups will be awarded.

For 1st Place routines, it is common for the choreographer to be called to the stage and given a monetary award. Top scoring solos may win, for example, a scholarship to an intensive or a gift certificate toward entry fees for the following regional competition season.

There are many other awards that can be given out during the awards ceremony. Check competition websites for specifics.

Choreographer reviews judges' scores and critiques of a solo routine.

JUDGES' SCORING

Don't take criticism personally. Each competition will have its own panel of judges with various expectations, critiques, and reactions to a dance routine. **"It's just three people's opinions" is often said.**

SCORESHEETS AND CRITIQUES

After a competition event, your studio owner/company director will receive judges' **scoresheets** for routines performed by the company dancers. In addition, they receive judges' **critiques**–either written, audio, or audio with video. Live critiques immediately after a performance are less common but do occur.

Your studio owner/company director will have a policy for how they deal with judges' scoresheets and critiques. He or she may limit with whom this feedback is shared. If shared with dancers, this will typically occur during weekly rehearsals for group routines or during scheduled rehearsals for solo/duet/trios routines. Parents may or may not be given access to scoresheets and/or critiques.

Critiques can be valuable for fostering continuous improvement. It can also be helpful for a dancer to hear feedback from someone (a judge) other than his or her choreographer. However, your studio may have reasons for not sharing them, including wanting to protect dancers and parents from potentially harmful comments or hurtful feedback from a biased judge.

Stay positive. The difference between 1st Place and 7th Place can be a handful of points, so keep your eye on the bigger picture! Dancers must stay focused and positive throughout the entirety of the competition—and afterward.

It's not all about the win. Don't worry so much about scores and awards. Being part of competitive dance is really about the experience, learning how to perform, receiving critiques, handling ups and downs, etc. There's so much more to gain than taking home a trophy.

TIPS FOR AFTER A COMPETITION

- Have your dancer remove makeup, hydrate, and rest.
- Unpack sweaty costumes and shoes at home.
- Organize costumes and accessories for the next competition weekend.
- Check your child's dance bag to see if something was left at the competition venue or was picked up by another dance family. You won't want to be surprised at the next competition when you realize you are missing something!

WHAT TO DO WITH ALL YOUR CHILD'S AWARDS?

Over the years, **pins, ribbons, plaques,** and **trophies** tend to pile up on you! So, what can you do with all of them?

- Keep them as keepsakes, especially the ones that have special meaning to you or your dancer.
- Place pins on the company jacket, lanyard, or dance bag
- Donate them to local theater companies, schools, or Special Olympics.
- Create a cork board with pins and ribbons.
- Buy or make a dance medal display (Check out Pinterest for ideas).

You can always take a picture of awards for posterity before parting with them!

"The two words information and communication are often used interchangeably, but they signify quite different things. Information is giving out; communication is getting through."

-SYDNEY J. HARRIS

© iStock photo / danr13

FOR DANCERS: COMMON STRESSORS AND HOW TO HANDLE THEM

Performing at competitions can give a dancer the jitters because of a variety of mishaps that can occur:

FORGETTING A COSTUME OR SUPPLIES—which is why having a checklist and reviewing it multiple times before packing is extremely important! Bringing along extra supplies and accessories can also come in handy; even if you don't need them, someone else might.

FORGETTING THE ROUTINE—which can happen to the best of us! Sometimes a dancer will forget the steps or placement onstage. Especially for young dancers, stage fright can cause them to freeze or run off stage, ending the performance abruptly. More seasoned dancers often have the skills and experience to improvise the dance until they remember the choreography. Rehearsing over and over is intended to make all dancers feel comfortable with and confident about their routines.

MUSIC GLITCHES—or other forms of technology's downside, can impede a routine. Technology, meant to make life easier, can sometimes trip up dancers where music is involved. Rare but realistic situations include when music doesn't start, stops in the middle of a routine, or belongs to another routine. If the music doesn't start or it belongs to another routine, the dancer can leave the stage until the music is sorted out. If music stops in the middle of a routine, dancers who continue to dance and complete their routine successfully should be commended; they show tremendous courage and professionalism by overcoming this obstacle.

COSTUME MALFUNCTIONING—which is known to happen. If the dancer is exposed, he or she must exit the stage and will likely laugh about the experience in the future. Otherwise, the show must go on—your child should just keep dancing! Dress rehearsal/ showcase should uncover potential issues that might occur at competitions, including wardrobe malfunctions.

(WO)MAN DOWN—is not just a battle term. When a team member in a group routine becomes unavailable at the last minute—due to illness or other reasons—the rest of the team must cope. This means having another dancer step in (supposing that he or she can learn the dance quickly enough to replace the absent dancer), having the choreographer quickly re-block the group formations in terms of pace and space, or performing a routine with a gap in performers. This issue can also occur if a dancer doesn't arrive on time… so **make sure your dancer is never late.**

NOT MEETING EXPECTATIONS—of the team, choreographer, family, and friends is a common concern for a dancer. Support and encourage your child, and **let the choreographer provide performance feedback.**

Although a "crisis" is very likely to occur at some point, keep in mind that these things happen to the best of us; deal with the situation with as much grace as possible. "This too shall pass," and there will be future opportunities to get it right. To keep mishaps in perspective, remember that the studio owner/company director and choreographers have probably seen and experienced it all!

NOTES

A WORD OF ADVICE ABOUT TIGHTS

PREVENTING RIPS

- Make sure the tights fit well—the tighter they are, the more vulnerable they are to snags and rips!
- Protect tights by putting them in a plastic zipper bag (don't leave them loose and vulnerable).

WHEN SNAGS AND RIPS HAPPEN—DON'T PANIC!

- If you can replace ripped tights, do it. If you didn't bring extras, ask a fellow dance mom if they have a pair your child can use.
- If you can't replace ripped tights, you'll need to deal with them! If the fabric is thick enough, you may be able to sew the rip using a needle and thread.
- If your child is expected onstage any minute and you don't have the time or tools to fix ripped tights more permanently, apply clear nail polish along the tear to contain the damage. For extra measure, spray the area with hairspray.
- Throw away tights that are irreparably damaged. Otherwise, later, you may pick them up and confuse them with a good pair of tights!

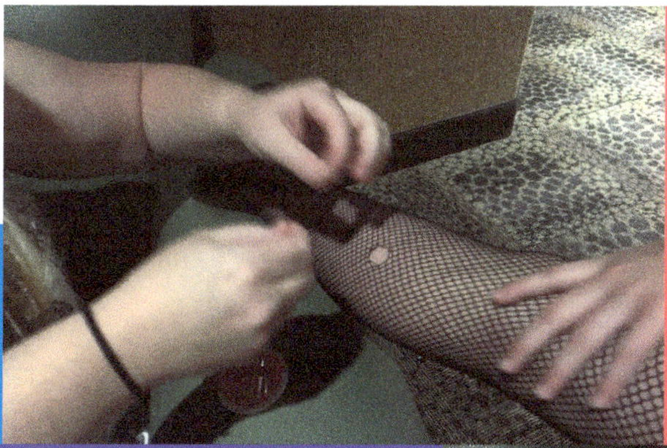

Sewing a rip in fishnet tights before going on stage.

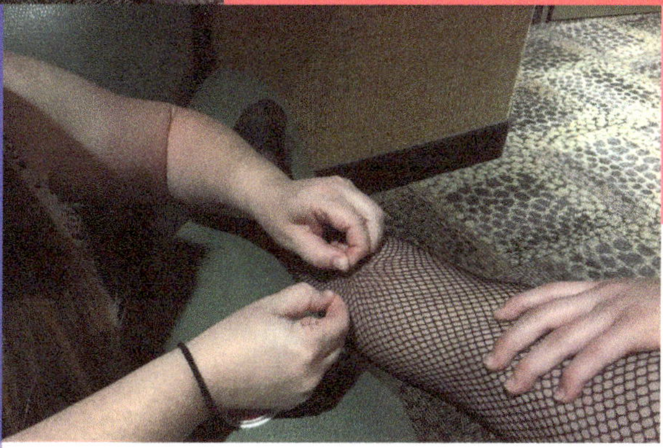

Note: Some studios have their company dancers wear tan tights under black fishnet tights which gives a polished, uniformed look and an extra layer of protection.

FOR PARENTS: TIPS FOR A STRESS-FREE COMPETITION

1. REMEMBER, YOU'RE PART OF A TEAM. Be positive and support everyone at your studio—encourage your dancer to do the same. Ask how you can help to make the event run smoother (e.g., with props, costumes, hair, etc.)—it's satisfying and fun to be part of the team's success. Assume positive intent regarding the actions of others and enjoy the team camaraderie!

2. BE RESPECTFUL—FOLLOW THE "GOLDEN RULE." Show respect to your studio members as well as other studio members, judges, and competition staff—in hallways, dressing rooms, in the auditorium, and backstage. The "Golden Rule" (do unto others...) is a beneficial approach, especially in the naturally exciting and intense circumstances of a competition. Respectful behavior on your part will mitigate the risk of negative, stressful interactions with others.

3. KEEP ANY NEGATIVE FEELINGS TO YOURSELF. Do not share with your child or others when you're upset with a dancer, staff member, or another dance parent. Your child is part of a team, and—especially during a competition when the stakes are high—it's important for him or her to stay focused on the team and during performances. Parents tend to become revved up at competitions, and you just might regret that you said anything controversial in the heat of the moment. If you have an issue with another person, show restraint and commit to resolving it after the event.

4. TALK TO THE PARENT, NOT THE CHILD. If you have an issue with another dancer that must be addressed, talk to his or her parent. It's not wise for an adult to confront a child, and such a situation is ripe for "papa bear" or "momma bear" to come out in defense of his or her child.

5. DO NOT CRITIQUE YOUR CHILD. Your job at a competition is to be your child's biggest supporter—be positive and feed your child's passion and enthusiasm. Putting pressure on children can break their spirits and impact their overall experience, which is counterintuitive—and you've spent too much time, energy, and money to get to this point. Leave instructions or critiques to the choreographer—that's his or her job.

6. ASSUME THAT ISSUES CAN BE RESOLVED. You and your team will no doubt experience a crisis or two (real or perceived) during a competition event. There are many ways to resolve issues that crop up, so take a deep breath and think logically about how to tackle them. Don't hesitate to seek help from other dance parents, if needed.

7. WIN & LOSE GRACIOUSLY. When your dancer wins, be humble. When your dancer does not do as well as expected, be proud. When other dancers win, be congratulatory—being gracious feels better than feeling jealous. And, through your behavior, your child will learn very valuable lessons.

NOTES

Photo Credit - JCM Photography

"I look at the dancers and I get the inspiration for the work from them."
– Graeme Murphy

DANCE CONVENTIONS

The dance convention is yet another realm in the universe of competitive dance. Conventions are basically large get-togethers where qualified faculty members—professionals within the dance industry—teach classes to students in a variety of dance styles. **This is a setting where dancers unite with instructors outside their home studio.**

Like dance competition companies, convention companies put on annual tours with **regional events** (also called "stops") in cities throughout the country, drawing dancers from the surrounding area. Most tours end with **a national event.** There are numerous convention tours across the U.S. with tour dates typically occurring between September and July.

Dance convention classes are **typically held in hotel ballrooms,** which are suitably spacious. The convention event typically **occurs over an entire weekend** and is **often combined with a competition.** When that is the case, some conventions may require dancers to compete in order to register for the convention workshop, while others may require dancers to register for the convention workshop in order to compete.

Most dance conventions offer instruction for a variety of genres including ballet, tap, jazz, hip hop, musical theater, and contemporary. However, there are some conventions which focus on a specific dance style—e.g., "Monsters Dance" (a hip hop convention) or "Tap Kids" (for tappers).

If your child is a company team member, he or she may be required to participate in one or more dance conventions during the dance year; check the company contract that you and your child signed at the beginning of the dance season.

» Some conventions require participation in all dance classes, in every genre. If not required, even if it's out of your child's comfort zone, he or she is encouraged to participate. Conventions are a time for dancers to take full advantage of opportunities to work with professional choreographers outside their home studio, meet new peers, and invest in their love of dance—just as you've financially invested in this convention as a dance parent.

THE BENEFITS OF A CONVENTION

CONVENTIONS OFFER

- An opportunity for your child to **make connections** with—and get noticed by—faculty who are currently working in the dance industry.
- A way for dancers to **gain influences and insight** from instructors beyond their studio.
- An occasion to **meet dancers from other studios and communities.**
- **An increased understanding of the professional dance world.**
- **Exposure to different dance styles and techniques.**
- A means for **learning how to audition.**
- **Photo-ops** with professionals and role models.
- The opportunity to receive **awards,** including class and convention scholarships.

POTENTIAL DRAWBACKS INCLUDE

- **Claustrophobic settings.** A convention will place many dancers in a limited space. It can get crowded and uncomfortable for some participants.
- **More competitiveness and comparisons.** Such an environment can highlight gaps in the technical and mental preparedness of some dancers; some children can't seem to find their comfort zone among so many talented peers.
- **Disappointment,** resulting from not being recognized via awards and scholarships.

TRICKS OF THE TRADE-How to keep scholarship numbers in good shape throughout the weekend.

Scholarship numbers affixed to dancewear can get damaged by an active dancer. Consider covering them with packing tape, laminating sheets, or clear shipping tape before they're pinned on your dancer.

THE STRUCTURE OF A CONVENTION

REGISTRATION

Many convention companies require participants to be registered through a dance studio. If you're thinking of going on your own (i.e., your child will attend the convention as an independent dancer), check with your studio or contact the convention company directly to see what options are available to you.

ARRIVAL AT THE VENUE

When you arrive at the convention venue, you'll want to check in and receive your child's **"scholarship" number** (a unique number that must be affixed to dancers' clothes with adhesive or safety pins so that they can be identified by the instructors). Also, pick up your dancer's **wristband**, required to access the workshop rooms. Pick up these items either at the registration table or from your studio representative who will hand them out to their registered dancers (check ahead of time for instructions).

As a parent, you can also pick up an **observer band** for yourself—these are wristbands that give parents of registered/paid dancers access into the workshop rooms to observe their children. Some conventions give wristbands as part of a dancer's registration fee, others sell them for an added cost (ranging from approximately $25 - $65). Purchases can be made prior to the event (your studio will usually order them for you) or at the time of the event.

Dancers gather at the convention venue to receive instructions, their scholarship numbers, and wristbands from their studio owner; parents also receive their observer bands.

Observer Band

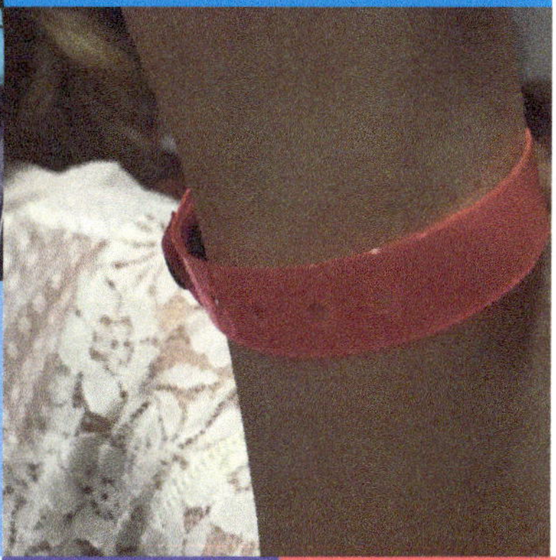

Dancers will wear a scholarship number (in this example, "420") for identification by the choreographer.

SHOULD YOU STAY IN THE WORKSHOP ROOM (WITH AN OBSERVER BAND) OR GO?

The answer depends from child to child and parent to parent. (Also, some convention companies and studios do not allow parent observers.)

CONSIDERATIONS FOR OBSERVING

- You don't mind the expense of a wristband.
- Your child has the maturity to focus on the instructors without your presence being a distraction.
- Your child will need your help in between workshop classes. After each workshop class, dancers usually change footwear, take a water or snack break, and take a trip to the bathroom. Although the studio staff members will either be dedicated to workshop rooms or travel from room to room looking after their students, they don't have time to give individualized attention to each child. For parents that do have observer bands, it doesn't put the responsibility of your child on them.
- Your child likes you to watch him or her and you want to observe your child being taught by the faculty members (and you can see what your child is getting out of your financial investment in the convention).
- You can always leave the room and reenter it when you desire.

If you decide to stay in the room and observe your child, be respectful of the instructor and dancers by being organized with your belongings and keeping quiet. Taking pictures and videos is typically not allowed during classes, so make sure you understand the convention rules for an observer.

CONSIDERATIONS AGAINST OBSERVING

- Some studios and conventions may not allow observers—making this an easy "decision."
- You'd like to save on the expense of a wristband.
- Your child has the maturity to remain focused on the instruction without your oversight.
- Your presence would be a distraction to your child.
- You have other children that require your time and attention outside the workshop room.

If you decide to not stay in the workshop room, make sure your child has the necessary supplies (e.g., footwear, water, snacks, adhesive bandages, pain medication, etc.) and that he or she has a way to contact you, if needed. Refer to the **Convention Packing Checklist** on page 142.

Some convention companies do not open classes to parent observation – this arrangement typically does not apply to the youngest dancers (e.g., Minis). The benefits include more focused students and more room for them to spread out.

SCHEDULE OVERVIEW

Prior to the event, the convention company will publish a detailed schedule on their website. Your studio should also be able to provide you with a copy of the schedule. Here is a sample convention schedule by Adrenaline Dance Convention:

Adrenaline Dance Convention schedule
Credit: Adrenaline Dance, Inc. | www.adrenalinedance.com

SCHEDULE HIGHLIGHTS INCLUDE

REGISTRATION/CHECK IN

At the beginning of the convention event, there will be a table set up for registration and check in. Here, you or your studio staff will make payments and pick up scholarship numbers and observer bands.

MASTER ("BONUS") CLASSES

Conventions may include one or more classes that are optional for dancers and provide them with an extra opportunity to work with "masters" in the craft. Attending these classes may furthermore give your dancer a boost when scholarships are considered, as work ethic, dedication, and passion are noted by faculty members.

OPENING CEREMONY–FACULTY INTRODUCTIONS & WARM-UP

Before the workshop classes start, there is usually an opening ceremony where all dancers meet in a single room and faculty introductions are made, followed by an official warm-up. This is typically a time of high energy and excitement, meant to energize the participants. When the opening ceremony is over, dancers will head to their first class.

Credit: Adrenaline Dance, Inc. | www.adrenalinedance.com

WORKSHOP CLASSES

Classes are usually one-hour long. Dancers are categorized in classes primarily by their age to account for their maturity and skill level, giving participants the most beneficial situation. (Generally, convention companies allow studio staff to decide whether to place a student by age or ability.) Each age group will be assigned to a separate room; the group should be indicated by a sign in front of each respective room to help dancers and parents orient themselves. Below is an example of how age level may be categorized; as always, check convention company websites for specifics.

MINIS	JUNIORS	TEENS	SENIORS
(5 TO 8)	(9 TO 12)	(13 TO 15)	(16 TO 19)

A dancer's age category is typically based on his or her age on the date of the convention. This is different from a conventional (non-convention) competition where the age is based on his or her age as of January 1st of the current dance year.

A workshop room is usually a large space with a dance floor surrounded by carpet. The room will be lined with chairs, used by observers during classes and by dancers during breaks (dancers are discouraged from sitting during the workshop). At the front of the room, a raised stage with audio equipment will be set up for the instructor.

Prior to the workshop, dancers should ensure that they're wearing the appropriate dancewear and footwear for the dance style of the workshop, and they should take time to warm-up. When the instructor walks in, he or she will head to the stage, signaling to the dancers that it's time to get started. The instructor will set up the music, make an introduction, and get the workshop started; he or she may also be accompanied by **convention assistants** who join him or her onstage to serve as an example and inspiration to the students.

Although the framework of classes may vary among conventions and dance genres, they typically begin with a few **warm-up exercises** and then transition to **learning a combination.** As the combination is taught, all dancers follow the instructor's lead. When the instructor signals that it is time, **dancers will be split into small groups** that will be called out to the floor to practice and perform what they just learned, one group at a time. Having smaller groups allows the instructor to have a better overview of the dancers and the opportunity to provide feedback.

From time to time, the instructors will jot down notes as the dancers perform. They are, in fact, noting the scholarship numbers of those dancers whom they believe excel at the routine. Toward the end of the scheduled class time, the instructors will call a select group of dancers—typically the ones noted on that piece of paper—to perform the routine in front of the other students. Sometimes, they will even call these dancers on the stage to serve as an inspiration to the class!

CLASS SCHOLARSHIPS

Faculty members at most conventions will award **class scholarships** in each of their classes to **students who excel or display great attitudes or work ethic.** Winners are typically announced and called up on stage during the closing ceremony. **Prizes** will vary among convention companies and may include free entry to their tour during the following dance season or money toward an intensive.

CONVENTION SCHOLARSHIP AUDITION COMBINATION CLASS

During this part of the convention, **dancers of each workshop level** (e.g., Minis, Juniors, Teens, and Seniors) **will learn a combination** which they'll perform during an audition in hopes of earning a convention scholarship. Although auditions are not mandatory, they are encouraged; they are great learning opportunities. Studio staff members are usually allowed to observe the class, while parents and other observers are not.

CONVENTION SCHOLARSHIP AUDITIONS

Following the audition combination class, dancers of each workshop level will head into an **audition for a convention scholarship**. Studio staff members are usually allowed to observe the audition, while parents and other observers are not.

During the audition process, the entire group of dancers will be split into smaller groups, perform the combination, and receive evaluation by convention faculty members **(male and female dancers are typically evaluated and awarded separately).** The typical duration of an audition is 15 minutes after they've learned the combo.

Winners are usually announced at the closing ceremony. **Prizes** will vary among convention companies and may include free entry to their tour during the following dance season or money toward an intensive.

COMPETITION

When a convention is combined with a competition, dancers typically compete on Friday and Saturday afternoons/evenings. For example, Minis and Juniors may compete on Friday, while Teens and Seniors compete on Saturday.

Competitions at conventions are typically unleveled (i.e., all dancers compete at the same entry level).

CHECK TO SEE IF THERE ARE **LIVESTREAMS** OF THE DANCE COMPETITIONS AND INFORM YOUR FRIENDS AND FAMILY MEMBERS SO THEY CAN WATCH YOUR CHILD'S DANCE PERFORMANCES, NO MATTER WHERE THEY ARE!

Dancers taking a lunch break

CLOSING SHOW AND SCHOLARSHIP AWARDS

The closing show at a convention is the culmination and celebration of the entire weekend and typically includes a faculty performance and the presentation of scholarship and other awards where winners are called up on stage. (The number of scholarships awarded varies depending on the convention's size and dancers' skill levels.) Most studios require dancers to stay through the closing ceremony to either accept a scholarship or award or cheer their fellow dancers who may become winners.

Revive and Adrenaline scholarship awards
Credit: Adrenaline Dance, Inc.
www.adrenalinedance.com

WHAT IS A CONVENTION ASSISTANT?

Some convention companies have an assistant program that allows young dancers to become part of their annual tour. This prestigious position generally involves assisting faculty, including demonstrating choreography on stage along with the instructor, as well as helping convention participants.

Assistants are known for strong technique, the ability to learn combinations quickly, and having friendly personalities. There are various ways for a dancer to become a convention assistant, including being recognized in a regional event (i.e., by earning an award of some type), being invited to audition for the position, or auditioning via online submission with video. Check convention websites for specifics regarding the process and requirements.

Once selected, convention assistants will participate in the convention's upcoming annual tour and are typically required to participate in a minimum number of cities.

Being a convention assistant is a great way to grow as a dancer and get to know (and become known within) the dance world.

» AFTER THE CONVENTION WEEKEND, YOUR CHILD WILL MOST LIKELY BE EXHAUSTED. DON'T FORGET TO PACK A PILLOW IN CASE HE OR SHE FALLS ASLEEP ON THE WAY HOME! «

PRIOR TO THE CONVENTION– A FEW REMINDERS

As a dance parent, here some steps you can take to enhance your child's and your own experience:

REGISTRATION

- If attending a convention as a scheduled event with your dance studio, studio staff should handle registration. If the studio has not scheduled a convention, but you'd like for your child to participate, your studio may handle the registration with the convention company for you. Otherwise, if your studio and the convention allow it, register on your own (independently) via the company website. Check to see if there are early registration discounts.
- Order an observer wristband to be allowed entry into classes to observe your child, if allowed.

ACCOMMODATIONS

- If traveling out of town to a convention, you'll likely need to book a hotel room unless you're staying with friends or relatives. (Studios typically don't book reservations for families.) Hotel availability can be limited, so **book reservations early.**
- **Hotel room "blocks"** are established for groups at a fixed, pre-negotiated rate. Check if the convention company has set up a block rate so you can make your hotel reservations at the special rate. Availability of these rooms is limited, so call and book early.

PACKING

- Large duffel bags take up a lot of space and are discouraged in convention rooms, so pack a suitcase for the weekend and **a small duffel bag or backpack for the convention classes.**
- **Label all your child's belongings.**
- Put a **luggage tag** with your child's name and phone number on your suitcase, duffel bag, or backpack.
- Don't pack too many regular **clothes** for your child—he or she will be in dancewear most of the weekend.
- Bring **swimwear**. Swimming at the hotel pool, whenever possible during the weekend, is a highlight!

DANCEWEAR PURCHASES

- Dancewear is often sold at conventions, so plan accordingly if you'd like to spend some money on purchases.

FOOD AND DRINKS

- To keep your dancer fueled and to keep costs down, bring healthy snacks and drinks.
- Consider packing nut-free items to be considerate of those with allergies.
- Avoid drinks and foods that can discolor dancewear.

TIPS FOR PARTICIPATING IN A CONVENTION

1. DANCER: REMEMBER THAT ATTITUDE COUNTS

- Dancers should display a **positive attitude,** ready to participate in classes for all dance genres.
- Being **teachable students** who **learn choreography quickly** will get dancers noticed—so will strong technique and dancing "full-out."
- Dancers should **refrain from sitting without permission, asking unnecessary questions, talking out of line, and distracting others** with unnecessary movements. Negative behaviors, such as crying and sulking, are noted by studio and convention faculty and are highly frowned upon.
- Dancers are expected to **display the utmost respect for faculty members and fellow dancers.** Instructors are fun and energetic, but they also take their task seriously!
- **Make a great first impression!** A convention is an opportunity for dancers to make life-changing connections.
- Dancers should **show their gratitude to the instructors** at the end of class.

2. DANCER: DRESS TO IMPRESS

- Have your child wear **appropriate dance clothes** to the convention classes. This includes a variety of dance styles: form-fitting leggings or shorts, sports bras or form-fitting tops and leotards. Loose tank tops and sweatpants might be appropriate for a hip hop class. Tights may be appropriate for ballet, but otherwise a leotard only is acceptable–dancers can get hot and sweaty! **Note: Some studios require a certain attire** for all dancers (e.g., all black dancewear or a black leotard with pink tights).
- Dancers should **look clean and polished** in a professional-looking outfit with hairpiece. As a general rule, hair should be kept off the face. Some parents buy new dancewear to boost their child's confidence, which carries into the class. Whatever the attire, your dancer should feel comfortable.
- If a dancer wants to get more easily noticed by the instructor, **select a style of dance attire that is unique to them** from day to day. Girls—usually the younger ones—might wear a colorful hairbow.
- **Apply (at least) a minimum amount of make-up.**
- **Wear studio or company spirit wear** when traveling to and from convention classes.
- Some conventions may require that dancewear (only) is not worn outside the workshop rooms. **Bring a cover-up, jumper, sweatpants, and/or sweatshirts** for your dancer.

3. DANCER: COME PREPARED

- Dancers should **be prepared to be challenged.**
- Dancers should be **well-rested, fed, and hydrated.**
- **Bring all your child's footwear** including ballet slippers, jazz shoes, tap shoes, socks, dance paws, and athletic shoes for hip hop.
- In many of the convention rooms, much of the space will be covered in carpet, so **dancers may prefer to wear socks,** especially for Jazz or Contemporary classes. Going barefoot is not recommended on carpet.
- Refer to the **Convention Packing Checklist** on page 142.

4. PARENT: PRIORITIZE SAFETY

- Conventions are busy with a lot of people around. Parental supervision of children is required to ensure their safety at the convention venue.

5. PARENT: MAKE TIME FOR MEALS

- In addition to the snacks and drinks you'll pack for a convention, plan to provide your child with a meal during the scheduled lunch break. Many parents make a trip to a local store or restaurant to grab their child's meal. A good meal will help keep your child's energy up during a long day of dancing.

6. PARENT: KNOW YOUR ROLE AND PROVIDE SUPPORT

- Buy an observer band for entry into convention classes to care for and observe your child.
- Bring something to keep yourself busy (a book, magazines, laptop, etc.).
- Don't be a distraction to the instructors or dancers.
- To give dancers the most amount of room to move, stay (with you and your child's belongings) as far back against the wall as possible.
- Don't take pictures or videos during workshop classes. Most instructors will let you take pictures of your child with them after a class has ended.

7. DANCER: KNOW HOW TO DEAL WITH COMPETITION

- During conventions, dancers can earn scholarships and awards, so the competition among dancers can be intense and nerve-wracking. Competitive emotions among dancers and teammates can emerge, so be prepared!
- Some convention tours are combined with a competition event. In this case—different from basic competitions—the age category for competition can be dependent upon the age of the dancer the day of the competition. Each competition company will have their own rules. Check competition websites for specifics.

CONVENTION PACKING CHECKLIST

In preparation for a convention, pack the following supplies in

DANCEWEAR & FOOTWEAR

- ☐ Form-fitted leggings or shorts, sports bras, form-fitting tops, leotards, loose tank tops, and sweatpants
- ☐ Socks
- ☐ Footwear for all dance genres including ballet slippers, jazz shoes, tap shoes, dance paw shoes, and athletic shoes
- ☐ Cover-up, jumper, sweatpants, and/or sweatshirts
- ☐ Company spirit wear (company jacket)

HAIR

- ☐ Brush/comb
- ☐ Hair pins/bobby pins
- ☐ Ponytail holders/elastic hair bands/ hair ties
- ☐ Curling iron/straightening iron
- ☐ Hair spray bottle with water
- ☐ Bun maker donut/Hairagami
- ☐ Colorful bows

MAKEUP

- ☐ Hanging mirror
- ☐ Makeup brushes
- ☐ Foundation/blush
- ☐ Mascara
- ☐ Lip gloss/lipstick

Label all your child's belongings by writing his or her name or initials with a black or gray Sharpie® on the tag in dancewear, footwear, costumes, tights, accessories,

MEDICINE CABINET/PERSONAL PRODUCTS

- ☐ Athletic tape/bandages
- ☐ Clear adhesive bandages of various shapes and sizes
- ☐ Blister bandages
- ☐ Ice packs
- ☐ Pain medicine
- ☐ Contact solution/eye drops
- ☐ Clear deodorant
- ☐ Toothbrush/toothpaste
- ☐ Feminine hygiene products
- ☐ Clothes and undergarments for leaving competition

OTHER SUPPLIES

- ☐ Sharpies®
- ☐ Safety pins of various sizes
- ☐ Small scissors/needle/thread
- ☐ Wet wipes/tissues
- ☐ Towel
- ☐ Pillow and blanket
- ☐ Accessories to warm up (foam roller, resistance band, etc.)
- ☐ Phone, phone charger
- ☐ Power strip for sharing outlet!
- ☐ Bathing suit
- ☐ Flip flops

FOOD & DRINKS

- ☐ Snacks (i.e., protein-rich food, nuts, fruit, vegetables)
- ☐ Water
- ☐ Rolling cooler for snacks and water

NOTES

Photo Credit - JCM Photography

"One can make no better investment than the cultivation of a taste for the beautiful, for it will bring rainbow hues and enduring joys to the whole life. It will not only greatly increase one's capacity for happiness, but also one's efficiency."

— ORISON SWETT MARDEN

ANNUAL DANCE COSTS FOR THE COMPETITIVE DANCER

If your child gets "bitten by the dance bug" and evolves into a competitive dancer, the cost to support this passion is not trivial. It's important to be aware of the associated expenses and prepare for them accordingly. Consider the **following two scenarios for a competitive dancer within a single dance year.**

	Scenario 1	Scenario 2
Recreational Classes	Unlimited Dancer*	Unlimited Dancer*
# Out-of-Town Competitions	3	3
# Out-of-Town Conventions	3	3
# Group Routines	6	3
# Solo/Duet/Trio Routines	1	None
Photogenic Award Entry	Yes	No
Title Award Entry	Yes	No

*Unlimited dancer package is common for competition dancers as team members are typically required to take a minimum number of classes which that is likely to exceed the unlimited limit. See page 6 for more details.

"Costs for dance families do not necessarily translate into profit for dance studio owners. The owners I've known usually start and maintain their business not for financial success but for the love of dance and sharing their passion with children. Some clients will say, "they're getting rich, they're charging me AGAIN for..." but what I focus on is planning and managing our own expenses rather than on how it affects the bottom line of the business. Again, the studio owners I've known are not 'rolling in the dough' from their dance business so without knowing the specifics, be aware of what your cost outlay is and manage it well." – B. Houben

The table on the following page details an example of costs.

PLEASE NOTE

- **THESE COSTS ARE ESTIMATES ONLY** and may not include incidental costs, such as competition pictures and videos, company pictures, etc. Costs **across regions and dance studios will vary.**
- Regarding dancewear and footwear, costs will similarly vary based on quality and where they are purchased. Keep in mind that each year these costs are likely to increase.
- The **total cost can be reduced** by opting for fewer group routines, opting out of solo/duets/trio routines, and not participating in extras such as Photogenic, Title, and Costume Awards. Between the two scenarios in example below, the estimated cost difference is $2,870.
- Depending on the studio, **dancers may be able to chose their own costumes** for solo/duet/trio routines, giving families the opportunity to spend what they like.
- Reviewing the overall cost for competitive dance might bring **"sticker shock."** However, if your child is passionate about dance, most parents will find a way to fund this passion. As well, it's important to keep in mind that other competitive sports (e.g., ice hockey, lacrosse, ice skating, baseball, etc.) for youths carry hefty costs as well. Sometimes, it's just the price we pay for elite levels of participation for our children.
- As you assess the overall cost of competitive dance, consider a studio's high overhead including space rental/lease and utilities, legal support, insurance, staff salaries, marketing expenses, office and other supplies, computer equipment and studio-management software, and more.
- To make payments more manageable, many studios will invoice families in smaller payments across several months, as opposed to payment in a lump sum.

> » DEPENDING UPON THE STUDIO, COMPANY MEMBERS MAY BE REQUIRED TO PURCHASE FOOTWEAR THAT IS WORN ONLY AT COMPETITIONS. «

Sample (not actual) annual costs for a competitive dancer for explanatory purposes*			
Item	**Description**	**Expense**	
RECREATIONAL DANCE COSTS			
Recreational Class	Nine months at $300 per month; dancer maximum (10+ classes)	$2,700	
Recital Costs	Recital fee ($65), 10 costumes ($75 each), 5 tickets ($15 each), program book ($10), package C recital pictures ($50), recital gift ($20)	$970	
ANNUAL RECREATIONAL TOTAL COST		**$3,670**	
COMPETITION DANCE COSTS			
Fixed Expenses			
Audition Fee	Due upon sign-up	$65	
Company Membership Fee	Warm-up jacket, jewelry, fees to cover hotel fees for staff, etc.	$300	
Competition Tights & Footwear*	Two pair of tights ($15 each) and jazz shoes ($40)	$70	
ANNUAL COMPETITION FIXED TOTAL COST		**$435**	
Variable Expenses (Depends upon # Routines and extras such as Title and Photogenic Awards)			
GROUP ROUTINES			
		Scenario 1	Scenario 2
Group Choreography	Due to choreographer at $25 per routine	$150	$75
Rehearsal	Nine months at $20 per month per routine	$1,080	$540
Costumes	Six costumes ($125 each)	$750	$375
Competition Entry Fees	Three competitions at $50 per routine	$900	$450
Hotel	Three weekends, Friday and Saturday at $200 per competition	$600	$600
ANNUAL GROUP ROUTINE TOTAL COST		**$3,480**	**$2,040**
SOLO ROUTINE			
Choreography	One solo routine	$150	$0
Rehearsal	Nine months at one hour per month ($65 per hour)	$585	$0
Costumes	One costume	$125	$0
Competition Entry Fees	Three competitions ($120 each)	$360	$0
ANNUAL SOLO/DUET/TRIO ROUTINE TOTAL COST		**$1,220**	**$0**
ADDITIONAL AWARDS ENTRIES			
Photogenic Entry	Three competitions ($30 for photo)	$90	$0
Title Entry	Three competitions ($40 each)	$120	$0
CONVENTION COSTS			
Fees	Three conventions ($245 each)	$735	
Hotel	Three weekends, Friday and Saturday at $200 per competition	$600	
ANNUAL CONVENTION TOTAL COST		$1,335	
ANNUAL COMPETITION AND CONVENTION TOTAL COST		**$6,680**	**$3,810**
ANNUAL RECREATIONAL, COMPETITION, AND CONVENTION TOTAL COST		**$10,350**	**$7,480**

*BEGINNER COMPANY DANCERS WILL MOST LIKELY SPEND LESS; THE MOST ADVANCED DANCERS IN THE STUDIO WILL LIKELY SPEND MORE.

SAMPLE COMPETITION BILL WORKSHEET

Below is sample **competition bill worksheet** that includes the costs of participating in three regional competitions and one national competition for a single dancer participating in one solo, one duet, eight group routines, and one production/line routine. These are only competition fees. Check your company contract, as some (if not all) competitions will likely be mandatory for all company dancers.

SAMPLE COMPETITION BILL WORKSHEET					(Excludes choreography, rehearsal and costume costs.)	
Entry Division	Performance/Age Division	Regional Comp 1	Regional Comp 2	Regional Comp 3	Nationals Comp 4	Total
Solo	Lyrical	$97	$115	$100	$130	$442
Duet	Musical Theater	$53	$80	$55	$85	$273
Group	Jazz – Junior	$40	$55	$45	$62	$202
	Lyrical – Junior	$40	$55	$45	$62	$202
	Lyrical – Teen	$40	$55	$45	$62	$202
	Jazz – Teen	$40	$55	$45	$62	$202
	Acro – Teen	$40	$55	$45	$62	$202
	Hip Hop – Teen	$40	$55	$45	$62	$202
	Tap – Teen	$40	$55	$45	$62	$202
	Musical Theater – Teen	$40	$55	$45	$62	$202
Production/Lines	Teen	$42	$60	$50	$69	$221
TOTAL		$512	$695	$565	$780	$2,552

TIPS TO REDUCE EXPENSES

REGARDING THE STUDIO

- Some studios offer **discounts** if you agree to pay with cash or check. Discounts may also be offered for upfront payments of recreational classes for the entire dance year.
- Some studios may waive the registration fee or offer tuition **discounts** for active duty military families.
- Pay your studio bill on time to **avoid late fees**.
- Check to see if your studio offers any **opportunities** in exchange for reduced recreational or other dance-related expenses (e.g., cleaning the studio or assisting with classes).
- **Booster clubs** and **fundraisers** can be a way to raise revenue to cover dance-related expenses; check to see if your studio offers these opportunities.

REGARDING RECITALS AND COMPETITIONS

- **Opt out of recital pieces** to reduce costume costs and attendance fees, if possible. For example, if your child is in six recreational classes and there is a recital piece for each class, sign up for four of your child's favorite classes, opting out of two.
- **Reduce the number of competition routines** in which your child participates.
- **Opt out of Photogenic, Title, and Costume awards at competition events.**

REGARDING DANCEWEAR, FOOTWEAR, AND COSTUMES

- **Write your child's name on dancewear and footwear,** as these items are often misplaced, and you will have to purchase new ones if they are lost. Labelling your child's items will make them identifiable, and if they are lost, more likely to be found and returned to you.
- An older dancer can **give away dancewear, footwear, and accessories** as they grow out of them; accept this kindness from others and practice it in turn.
- Make purchases with **online discount dancewear companies**; sign up for mailing lists to receive offers.
- When feasible, choose competition **costumes that are less expensive**.
- **Make your own costumes** for solo, duet, and trio routines.
- Search **eBay** for new and used costumes. **Consider consignment or used costume sales.** Check websites and social media (e.g., there may be a Facebook group that facilitates used costume sales).
- **Embellish your child's costumes, tights, and accessories** rather than purchasing these items already stoned.
- Get a group of dance parents together for a bulk, online order to **avoid shipping fees.**
- **Buy supplies (e.g., bobby pins, elastic hair ties, etc.) in bulk** at reduced prices.
- Keep an eye out for **in-store and online holiday (and other) discounts**.

REGARDING LOGISTICS

- For out-of-town conventions and competition events
  - Check into **"block" hotel rates**, which are less than normal rates.
  - **Share hotel rooms** with another dance family to divide the costs.
  - **Sign up for hotel loyalty programs to accumulate rewards** (e.g., free room upgrades, free stays, etc.)—the points you earn add up over time.
  - Select a hotel with **complimentary breakfast.**
- **Carpool** with fellow dancers to and from the studio, conventions, and competitions to split the costs.
- **Prepare snacks and meals ahead of time. Food purchased at** the grocery store is much less expensive than eating out and buying at convenience stores.

© Can Stock Photo Inc./xilius

NON-FINANCIAL COSTS

Financial costs are tangible and obvious; we can tie them to a dollar. Non-financial costs, however, are less transparent and can have a bigger impact on your family than anticipated. Depending on what your dancer's commitments are, such costs can include

- Limited time with family (dinners together throughout the week are at risk)
- Limited time for other extracurricular activities such as marching band, volleyball, cheerleading, etc.
- Limited time for traditional summer activities such as vacations, camps, etc.
- Time commuting with your child (that could be spent elsewhere)
- The impact on schoolwork and homework
- The impact on other children in your family
- Potential emotional effects of being in a competitive environment
- Sidestepping common childhood activities (e.g., skiing, skateboarding, rollerblading, etc.) to prevent potential injuries.

During the week, many dancers find themselves doing homework in the car driving to and from the dance studio, during breaks in between classes, in the evening after classes, or early in the morning before school. Weekends are a great time to do homework for the upcoming week.

"Our daughter–a competitive dancer–was in middle school when she realized that she was missing out on her school's football games during the week. School sports participation conflicted with her dance schedule. She felt a true conflict between her love of dance and her desire to engage in school activities. I learned that this is a fairly common predicament. The advice I was given from many with similar experiences is that most adults will never regret dancing but they do regret quitting dance. I was advised to encourage our daughter to keep going while offering her the opportunity to cut back on her dance commitment to make more room for her healthy desire to spend time with school friends and activities."

– B. Houben

NOTES

Photo Credit - JCM Photography

Photo Credit –JCM Photography

"You dance love, and you dance joy, and you dance dreams. And I know if I can make you smile by jumping over a couple of couches or running through a rainstorm, then I'll be very glad to be a song and dance man."

— GENE KELLY

Photo Credit - DancePixs by Acentric Video

THE GUYS: BOY DANCERS AND DANCE DADS

MALE DANCERS

Boys add to the diversity of a dance studio, and they're just as welcome as their female peers! Although today there are more boys than ever in the world of recreational and competitive dance, they are generally still far outnumbered by girls. Due to their limited number, therefore, they often get key roles in dance routines. Male dancers are also standouts at conventions, including moments when the choreographer might call out all boys to the dance floor to perform a class routine.

On that note, here are some of the most unique and important factors to keep in mind regarding male dancers:

- Whether at the studio or recital, competition or convention venues, boys won't necessarily have their own dressing area. They may be expected to change in the men's restroom or to come already dressed. A changing curtain or changing tent might be handy alternatives.
- Recital and competition costumes are simpler (e.g., a white shirt paired with black pants) and generally less expensive. Also, there are (generally) no makeup or special hairstyle requirements.
- Boys will focus on developing their core, as well as lower- and upper-body strength to enable them to physically lift other dancers more easily.
- Ballet can give boys an edge in sports, helping them develop fitness, great core strength and agility, while helping them master their balance.
- Boys may not have the natural turnout and flexibility for splits that girls have, so they may need to work harder to achieve these skills.
- Dance is not a traditionally-held activity for boys, which may lead to social tension.

> "My husband always says to our daughter, 'Just go out there and enjoy yourself, have fun girl' – and he means it! A great reminder of what it's really all about!"
>
> – B. Houben

DANCE DADS

Dads, like moms, play an integral role in providing support and encouragement to their dancing children, as well as being there for them physically and emotionally to assist in any way possible. Specifically, dads can be very helpful in getting their male dancers ready for the stage—whether in a dressing room, restroom, at home, or in a hotel room before the recital or competition—and to also assist the studio staff in the situating and transporting of props. There's even a phrase for this role—a "Prop Dad"—which many dance dads take pride in.

A PROP DAD IS TYPICALLY RESPONSIBLE FOR

- Building props and scenery for the stage
- Loading and unloading props and scenery to and from recital and competition locations
- Placing props on the stage at the recitals and competitions before the routine is performed (and removing them afterward)

In celebration and recognition of dance dads, some studios offer a daddy-daughter dance that can be performed at recitals and regional or national dance competitions.

> *"My father has always been my hero."*
>
> — GREGORY HINES

NOTES

Photo Credit - Danielle Trina Photography

Photo Credit - Stacey Glasco

"You have to dance unencumbered. There's no other way to move. The idea of dance is freedom. it is not exclusiveness, it's inclusiveness."

— JUDITH JAMISON

PROMOTING HEALTHY RELATIONSHIPS

As noted in the beginning of this book, one of the many benefits that results from the world of dance—recreational and competitive—includes the forging of friendships and bonds that spark within these environments. Once you find yourself surrounded by a committed and close-knit Dance Family, you may wonder how you used to get by without them. Getting to know fellow dancers, families, and studio staff is a worthwhile endeavor, opening many doors and introducing you and your child to many incredible people.

It's important to remember that all human interactions aren't without their inevitable sources of conflict. Learning how to understand and deal with conflicts is important for establishing and maintaining healthy relationships. Competitive dance requires a commitment of time, energy, and money. It demands emotional balance. You and your dancer will come in contact with people that have a variety of personalities, attitudes, backgrounds, and expectations. You and your dancer will have to learn to cope, accept, or deal with all of them. Dance creates an environment where competition—with all of its many highs and lows—is at play, proving a very strong variable in the whole equation of progress, communication, and success.

Above all, remember that the competitive spirit applies to parents and studio staff just as much as it applies to dancers.

COMPETITIVE FEELINGS

Most competitive dancers are serious about their craft; the act of competing, in any scenario, demands determination, ambition, and self-confidence. So naturally, **competitive dancers want to be the best they can;** they show up to do well—to win—which means beating others. This goal in and of itself puts a lot of pressure on everyone involved. It is especially relevant for the solo entry division, which gives dancers a unique opportunity to shine as individuals—and means that many team dancers within the same studio (who are peers and may even be close friends) will compete against each other as they take the stage and **strive for personal excellence and success.**

Another common source of tension among dancers ensues when they are not cast or chosen for a routine, or possibly when they are not made a front-row-dancer or the "star" (in which case they may complain by saying something along the lines of, "Nobody wants to pay attention to me!" or "I'm stuffed in the back in this routine!"). This can be hard to cope with, but these situations will help children learn that successes and opportunities must be divided among team members, must be earned, and are not always as easy to come by. It is a learning opportunity for children to accept and work through disappointments, and it can be something that helps them appreciate the good times while planning more determinedly for future improvements.

The inherent conflicts within a competitive environment can either flare up or snuff out, depending on the people involved. Remember that as a dance parent, you have incredible influence to encourage, uplift, and motivate your child in positive ways.

DIFFERING PERSONALITIES AND EXPECTATIONS

Goals and expectations between dancers and their parents or other family members will vary. Just so, the personalities, expectations, and goals of all dance families within the same studio, region, competition, or convention will differ as well. Some will strive to take their skills and passion to a professional level, while others will be involved in competitive dance for the multitude of other benefits derived from dance training and team participation. Serious dancers may survey other dancers and judge whether their teammates are "pulling their weight" and taking dance excellence seriously. These are common dynamics found within a competitive dance environment.

As with life in general, gossip, jealousy, and unreliable friends can cause problems for both children and parents within a competitive dance environment. Child dancers may not have the maturity to modulate their feelings; they can be very sensitive when experiencing hurts or slights as they arise. As a parent, recognize this risk and position yourself to support your child and enlighten him or her about dealing with these realities. **Teach your child to not give up;** at the dance studio, everything is fluid, and tough times are likely to come and go. Learning to deal with difficulties like this at a young age will help prepare children for adulthood.

PARENTAL OVER-INVOLVEMENT

Parents can be very involved in the progress of their child's training—to the point where the involvement becomes unhealthy. **It's important to find a balance.** When competitive dance demands such a high investment and there's a lot at stake, it makes sense that a dance family will want to garner the most from this investment. At the same time, an overly-high level of engagement might lead to overly-involved parents who attempt to step into the roles of instructors, choreographers, and other dance parents.

Children often assume their parents' behavior, thoughts, and language. Typically, children just want to dance and have fun, but their own attitudes and motives can be influenced when their parents are critical of the studio and other dancers and parents. If there is strong studio leadership, anything damaging to the overall health and success of the studio will be addressed and resolved.

BALANCING RELATIONSHIPS AS A DANCE PARENT

Whether interacting with the studio staff, other dance parents, or dancers, the best thing to do is always **strive for positive relationships** to enhance your experience (and your child's) and to mitigate conflicts. Your family's dance journey can be long and paved with many challenges and twists. It can be difficult—if not downright impossible—to repair burnt bridges once trust is lost. Parents who feel hurt—especially on behalf of something that was done or said to their children—can hold very strong grudges or be wary of opening up to fellow dance families.

Keeping things in perspective goes a long way, so consider the following–

STUDIO STAFF

- Dance studios ideally cater to many students and parents, requiring a great deal of the staff's time, care, and attention. Studio staff members juggle many activities including profit and loss management, choreography, scheduling, and conflicts—not to mention their own families, extra work obligations, and interests. **Imagine being in their shoes** for a day before judging their motives and actions.
- As with life in general, the dance world can be political and fraught with agendas and power-struggles. There is an expected protocol in terms of behavior. **Choose your battles** and consider what's truly important to your family.
- Be cognizant of your role as a dance parent and that of the staff. **Your job is to support; their job is to lead, teach, advise, instruct, revise, improve, critique, and choreograph routines.** Choose a studio where you have faith in the staff and trust their decisions in all things dance-related.
- Remember that, as in any professional environment, **studio decisions are typically made for the greater good** and aren't intended to be a personal affront to you or your child.
- Learn the **preferred method for communicating** with studio staff; catching them in between classes can be hectic and produce undesired results due to their limited time and attention.
- The business model for dance studios is a tricky one. Some staff members are even volunteers, and almost all are in it for the love of dance. **Don't assume the owner(s) are making a profit off your investment** in your child's dance.
- As questions will naturally arise, whenever you are confused or concerned, always **approach the staff in a polite and constructive manner.**

YOUR CHILD

- Don't underestimate the importance of your **child's social health and attitude** at the dance studio—it can make or break his or her experience and reaction to dance in general.
- Stay tuned to your **child's emotions and interest levels.**
- Encourage your child to be a "good citizen" by limiting gossip and negative talk, **being respectful of studio staff and peers, and having a strong work ethic.**
- **Encourage and support your child** no matter how he or she performs in the studio or on the stage.
- Remember that **children are all different** and achieve growth and success at different times in life. Resist comparing your child with others, and don't let him or her compare him or herself to anyone else. Consider the long-term vs. single event (e.g., a competition) in your child's dance journey, and help him or her to keep things in perspective.
- Remember—it's always about your child! **You are your child's advocate, cheerleader, and number one fan!**

DANCE PARENTS AND OTHER DANCERS

- Keep in mind that **people have different perspectives and expectations;** understand yours and stay laser-focused on your path to avoid judging others and mitigate conflict. Don't judge or criticize their outlooks or goals.
- Remember that competitive dance requires a **significant investment in terms of time, energy, and money.** It's logical that each dance family wants to make the most out of this investment. Competitive attitudes will be the norm, and they're acceptable as long as they're healthy. Again, avoid judging others and stay focused on your family's own goals and objectives.
- **Using social media to air grievances** or brag about your child can, for obvious reasons, backfire and bring about unwanted reactions from studio staff, fellow dance parents, and dancers. Think twice about why you're publicly posting something and what consequences it might bring your family.
- **Don't reprimand another child.** If necessary, speak directly to studio staff or the child's parents.

GENERAL TIPS

- **Be respectful** to studio staff, dance parents, dancers, and competitors.
- **Stay out of the drama**—because it will surely exist—and focus on being your child's strongest advocate.
- **Don't gossip or speak ill about anyone** involved with the dance studio.

"My husband, daughter and I went to visit a friend in the Las Vegas area recently who had told me for years about their neighbor, a highly accomplished competitive dancer—her name is Madison. When we arrived at her home, we were introduced to Madison and the first thing she did was give my daughter a hug because she knew our daughter is also a dancer. This is the camaraderie in the dance world that is worth it all!"
–B. Houben

TO STAY OR GO

Once your family becomes a part of the studio dance family, leaving for another studio (for better training, lower costs, or different opportunities) becomes an increasingly challenging reality. The thought of leaving, especially for your child, can become unthinkable. Many times, families will forgo a change to stay with their friends and dance family.

Reasons why people leave a dance studio–

- Change to another studio to better meet needs in terms of environment, culture, training, and programs
- The child stops dancing altogether to do other things

Each family needs to assess their own priorities.

> *"Opportunity dances with those who are ready on the dance floor."*
>
> –H. JACKSON BROWN, JR.

OPPORTUNITIES FOR GRADUATING SENIORS AFTER HIGH SCHOOL

While this book caters to families of child dancers, it should go without saying that this can be just the beginning of a lifetime endeavor and passion. With years of dance training, there are numerous paths dancers can take after high school. Whether your child chooses a career in the field of dance, what he or she has learned during the dance journey can arm him or her with lessons and skills that are transferable to all careers and aspects of life. Below are just some avenues to take into consideration if your child still wants to actively pursue dance as a profession or hobby:

- Join a **conservatory** (a rigorous training curriculum for students seeking dance as a career, focused on the arts)
- Enroll in a **college dance program**
- Enroll in a **college program for sports medicine or physical therapy**
- Join a **professional dance company**
- Become a **faculty of a convention company**
- Become a dance **instructor** or **choreographer** at a dance studio or public school
- Open a dance studio/**become a studio owner**
- **Write for dance magazines or blogs**
- Become a **Rockette**
- Become a **professional cheerleader**
- **Make or design dance costumes**
- **Fundraise** for the performing arts
- Get involved in dance **marketing**
- Become a **cruise line** performer
- **Dance** on Broadway, at themed parks, in Las Vegas shows, or in summer stock productions

"The Theater Arts Preparatory School (TAPS) is a six-month trade school for dancers designed specifically for the job market. Currently almost 70% of our dancers are working in the industry."
—Don Mirault, President

"A dancer in our studio, now 17, was told when she was nine that she wasn't good enough to be on company. She is now going on to a professional career in dance. She is amazing, one of the best dancers I've ever seen. This is a great reminder to never let anyone put limitations on your child!"
- B. Houben

ONLINE RESOURCES

There is a tremendous amount of dance-related information online and on social media. Below are some of the many online resources that may help in your quest to navigate recreational and competitive dance.

FOR INFORMATION ABOUT CONVENTION AND COMPETITION COMPANIES

- Go to **www.dancecompetitionhub.com** to access dancer, parent, instructor, and studio owner reviews for competition and convention companies.
- Go to **www.danceinforma.com** as a resource for current, dance-related information; click on "Competitions and Conventions" to find company descriptions, tour dates, and contact information.
- Go to **www.dancecomps.com** to search for dance competitions in your area.
- Go to **Facebook, Twitter,** and **Instagram** to search the respective convention or competition company names and see what's in their feed. "Like" and "follow" to see their posts; it's amazing how much you can learn!

FOR ONLINE SOURCES RICH WITH DANCE-RELATED INFORMATION

- **Tututix:** www.tututix.com
- **Ballet Talk for Dancers:** dancers.invisionzone.com
- **All things Dance Blog:** www.conservativedancewear.blogspot.com
- **Your Daily Dance:** www.yourdailydance.com
- **Dance.com:** www.dance.com
- **Bitten by the Dance Bug:** www.bittenbythedancebug.com
- **YouTube:** www.YouTube.com: search online videos that demonstrate how to apply makeup and hair styles for dance competitions, recitals, and much, much more!

FOR INFORMATION ABOUT DANCE NEWS, AUDITIONS, JOB LISTINGS, AND MORE

- **Dance Informa:** www.danceinforma.com
- **Dance Magazine:** www.dancemagazine.com

NOTES

Photo Credit - Teresa Lee Photography

Photo Credit - Lisa Blakeley Gale

"The one thing that nobody else has is you. Your voice, your mind, your story, your vision. So write and draw and build and play and dance and live as only you can." –NEIL GAIMAN

JUST THE BEGINNING...

Some children will start out with a single dance class, get "bitten by the dance bug," and evolve into serious recreational or competitive dancers. Whatever the path they follow or however far they travel, they are sure to benefit from the many advantages of dance, ranging from physical health and mental growth to character development and social outreach, making this performance art an extremely worthwhile endeavor. The benefits of dedication to a child's growth and interest in dance are abundant and meaningful. Dancers will always remember the studio(s) they traversed during their formative, childhood years.

Navigating the universe of recreational and competitive dance, with all its complexities, is not a simple process. The ideal scenario is when the demands are met with parents and students who are informed, prepared, and organized. After reading this book, now equipped with a greater understanding of the basics and beyond, I hope you continue exploring the special world of children's dance.

Wishing you good luck and happy toes,

B. Houben

GLOSSARY OF TERMS

Acro: short for "Acrobatics." This dance genre combines classical dance technique with tumbling and acrobatic technique such as walkovers, handsprings, and aerials.

Across the Floor Work: steps executed in repetition and/or combinations of varying length as dancers move across the floor. Sometimes known as "diagonals."

Adjudication: when dancers are judged, evaluated, and receive a score during a dance competition.

Aerial: an Acrobatic skill where a cartwheel or front walk over is performed without the dancer's hands hitting the floor.

Audition: an event where a dancer shows off skills and talent to a panel of judges who will decide if a dancer is qualified to join a competitive company or team.

Barre Work: exercises to warm up the body and build the technique needed to work in center floor and across the floor. The barre is a handrail providing support.

Blinging: embellishing a costume with rhinestones, sequins, lace, and fringe.

Block Hotel Rates: hotel room "blocks" that are established for groups at a fixed, pre-negotiated rate.

Blocking or Spacing: the placement of dancers on a stage; dancers are directed to stand in a particular location and instructed to move up or down stage or to the right or left of the stage until the choreographer is satisfied with the dancers' placement in relation to the audience.

Call Time: the time dancers are due at a performance venue for recital or competition events.

Center Floor Work: steps executed center floor in repetition and/or combinations of varying length in the center of the room.

Choreographer: creates individual and group dance routines and performances including selecting the genre, song, costume, props, and lighting. Performances can include recital, showcase and competition pieces.

Cleaning: refers to polishing a routine and making it "cleaner" in terms of the quality of dance movements and for the clarification of physical spacing and timing. This can include ensuring that all dancers perform on the same counts, fine-tuning the position of arms, correcting tricks such as leaps and turns, etc. The routine is broken down into smaller sections and worked until it's "clean."

Competition *(Dance)*: an event where individuals and groups perform a dance routine in front of a panel of judges.

Combination *("combo")*: an integral part of a dancer's day-to-day training. A series of dance steps are linked together in a sequence and performed to music. Combos are taught by a lead-by-example method–the teacher demonstrates the steps and the dancers execute them. The purpose of combos is to develop memorization and choreography skills and to prepare dancers for the stage where they'll perform longer pieces that can be interpreted as a series of combos.

Convention *(Dance)*: an event where faculty, currently working in the dance industry, teach in various styles of dance.

Convention Assistants: young dancers who assist faculty during annual convention tours, including demonstrating choreography on stage along with the instructor, as well as helping convention participants.

Convertible Tights: tights that have an opening in the bottom of the foot, so they can either be worn over the dancer's foot or off the foot at the ankles (as footless tights). Also known as "transition" tights.

Dress Rehearsal: the rehearsal before the routine goes on stage in either a recital or competition. Also known as a "mock" rehearsal, when costumes, hair and makeup are set so that the choreographer and staff members can fully appraise what's going to go onstage.

Duet (also known as "Duo"): a dance routine with two dancers, can be a mix of boy and girl dancers.

E6000: glue used to "bling" costumes with stones.

Full-Out: to perform a routine with full energy and effort.

Gross: represents approximately 144 stones, of the same size, in a package.

Group Routine: a dance routine with four or more dancers.

Hairagami™: a hair tool for creating a bun.

Independent Dancer: a dancer who performs solo routines at competitions as a registered independent dancer, not under a dance studio or choreographer's name.

Intensives: rigorous dance training programs designed for motivated dancers and aspiring pre-professional and early-career dancers; the're typically held during summer, winter, or summer breaks, and taught by either studio teachers or master instructors.

Jazz Shoes: dance shoes worn during jazz and musical theater class and performances.

Marking: performing a dance routine at full speed to the music while using smaller, less energetic movements. Marking saves energy while allowing the dancers to focus on the timing of the movements with the music.

Musicality: the degree to which a dancer can translate or render music through movement. It's how well the dancer becomes "one" with the music.

Observer Band *(Convention)*: wristbands purchased by parents of registered dancers, allowing them into the workshop classes.

Oversplits: an exercise that extends regular splits, greater than 180 degrees, by elevating the front or back leg while in a split to increase flexibility. It is also seen in leaps where the dancer's split is greater than 180 degrees.

Privates: classes a dancer takes alone with a teacher or choreographer for one-on-one dance training sessions or to learn, rehearse, or clean a solo/duet/trio routine.

Prop: an item used on stage to enhance a performance and help in telling the narrative of the dance. Examples of props include a chair, a hand fan, a block, a swing, a mop, a large clock, etc.

Recital: an event, put on by a dance studio, where students perform to show their progress throughout a dance year.

Recreational *("rec")* Dancer: a dancer who takes recreational dance classes such as Ballet, Tap, Jazz, and Hip Hop. Learning the basics and a non-Competitive Dancer.

Rehearsal: preparation for a recital or competition event, working out all the details including costuming, props, spacing, and lighting.

Routine: a series of steps and movements (choreography) that dancers perform to a piece of music.

Scholarship number: a unique number that convention dancers will affix to their clothes with a safety pin so they can be identified by the dance instructors.

Scratch: an entry that is "scratched" is when the dancer doesn't perform their scheduled routine due to injury, illness, or other reasons.

Showcase: an event where a studio puts on a performance without the element of competition, or a full-dress rehearsal prior to a dance company's first competition.

Solo: a dance routine with a single dancer (soloist).

Stage Parent: either a stage mom or a stage dad (although a mother of a dancer is more likely to fulfill this role); supports the studio by managing dressing room activities and dancers' performance readiness, as well as escorting ("running") the dance groups to and from the stage and dressing room before and after their numbers are performed. "Stage Mom" is used interchangeably with "Dance Mom."

Stoning: embellishing a costume with rhinestones.

Title: an award given at a competition to a soloist (a dancer who performs a solo routine), separate from the adjudication score. Although some competitions automatically enroll all dancers for this award, most competitions require pre-registration accompanied with a separate entry fee.

Toe Spacers: an accessory to pointe shoes, small pads placed between toes to help prevent bunions by keeping the big toe in proper alignment.

Trio: a dance routine with three dancers; routine can be a mix of male and female dancers.

Troupe: a group of dancers that perform in competitions; also known as "team" or "company."

Turnout: the ability to rotate the legs outward from the hips, allowing the knee to align correctly over the foot. This rotation is supported by proper placement of the knees and feet and all adjoining muscles and muscular makeup from the hips and abdomen down through the feet—and the strength to hold the rotation.

Photo Credit - Teresa Lee Photography

RESOURCES, REFERENCES, AND CREDITS

The following companies graciously provided permission for their product and/or brand to be included in "Bitten by the Dance Bug."	
Acting for Dancers	Sarah and J. Brinson, Founders
Adrenaline Dance, Inc.	Amber Mills, Convention Manager
ADAPT and Signature Dance Inc.	Andrea Foley, Assistant to Brian Foley
Ajoy LLC	Shine Liu, CEO
AllAboutDance.com	Laura Guerra, Senior PR Specialist
Apolla Performance Wear	Brianne Zborowski, Co-Founder & CEO
Ballerina Boutique	Caitlin Hopwood, Owner
Ballet Strap	Suzana Palaic, Owner
Barefoot Images by Jen	Jen Rauchut, Owner
BDancewear.com	Cyndi Marziani, CEO
boysdancetoo.	Michael Colluci, Owner
Bravo! National Dance and Talent Competition	Brendan C. Buchanan, Executive Director and Owner
Capezio	Amanda Lederman, Social Media Coordinator
Conservativedancewear.blogspot.com	Alyson Tyler, Owner
DADesignsDancewear	Dennette Nakamura, Owner
Dance Pixs	Adam Reynolds, Owner
dancecomps.com	Daniel J. Graham, CEO/Principal
DanceSupplies.com	Kory Barrett, Vice President
Dancewear Corner	Jonathan Demott, President
Details Dancewear	Aline Ross, GM
Discount Dance Supply	Laura Guerra, PR
Diva Dolly	Jennifer Luongo, CEO
DJO, LLC	Leda Buster, Digital Marketing Solutions Manager
dot2dance	Susie Bradshaw, VP
Dream Duffel	Robert W. Johnson, COO
Dreamtime Creations	Michael Hervieux, Director of Online Operations
Eclectic Products	Teresa Morgan, Senior Product Manager
Five Dancewear	Lisa Wilson, Director of Operations
Flex Express	Stephen Helms, Operations Manager

Freshify Inc.	Patricia Moser, Founder
From Our Hearts to Your Toes	Amanda Milberg, Founder
Get Dancewear	Kara McKee, President
Glam'r Gear™	Sanny McKelvey, Co-Founder
Grit Inc.	Jo-Anne Chadwick, VP Finance
Hairagami Company	Nicholai Martinsen, COO
Inspired Designs Costumes LLC	Susanne Harvey, Owner
JCM Photography	Carmen Morales, Owner
Jo + Jax	Reza Fakhrieh, CEO/President
Just for Kix	Justin Heitkamp, Director of Catalog
King Shots, Inc.	Richard King, President
KNKMiami	Wilhelm Kopke, CEO
Ktrna	Ryan Cyphert, President
Level Up Dance Supplies	Alyson Tyler, Owner
Pack2Rack	Kara McKee, President
Racnroll	Sharon Middup, Director
Rhinestone Guy	Jeffrey and Carmit Brandt, Owners
Rhinestoneshop.com	Jason Pistiner, Attorney for Rhinestoneshop
Satin Stitches Ltd.	Deborah Nelson, President
Simply Caddy	Cathie Wrona, Owner
Skaraskins Photography	Tim Skaraskins, Owner
Stagestep	Bill Goldberg, Director of Operations
Sugar and Bruno	Steve Powers, V.P.
Summit Dance Works	Lyndzi Barnes, Executive Director
The Spin Spot™	Angela Pineda-Kyle, Owner
Sweet Feet LLC	Jeanette Wilson, Owner/President
The Theater Arts Preparatory School (TAPS)	Don Mirault, Owner
THINX	Maeve Roughton, Head of Content
Traveling Tutus	Jenna Fleetwood, President/Founder
Tututix.com	Mollie Durbin, Marketing Director
Whirl-A-Style	Lois Sonstegard, President
Y.P.A.D.	Joseph Zanovitch, Director

NOTES

NOTES

NOTES

NOTES

NOTES

NOTES

NOTES

NOTES

NOTES

NOTES

NOTES